FIRST PRINCIPLES

OF

POPULAR EDUCATION

AND

PUBLIC INSTRUCTION.

By S. S. RANDALL,

SUPERINTENDENT OF PUBLIC SCHOOLS OF THE CITY OF NEW YORK.

NEW YORK:

HARPER & BROTHERS, PUBLISHERS,

FRANKLIN SQUARE.

1869.

TO THE

HON. HENRY BARNARD, LL.D.,

COMMISSIONER OF EDUCATION OF THE UNITED STATES,

This Little Volume is respectfully inscribed, as a humble contribution to that great cause in which we have both been so long co-laborers, and to which the best energies of our lives have been devoted.

TABLE OF CONTENTS.

INTRODUCTORY.

If there be one subject which, more than any other, may be regarded as of paramount importance to the permanent well-being of a country like ours, it is that of the education of its successive generations of citizens. It has been well said that "Intelligence is the life of Liberty." In a government where the masses of the people possess or control all the functions and powers which are elsewhere conferred upon hereditary sovereigns, it is essential, not only to its own stability and welfare, but to the highest and most cherished interests of every individual comprising the community, that these high powers should be delegated to and exercised only by the enlightened, the wise and the good.

The following pages are offered to the public as the conclusions upon the several subjects discussed, resulting from an experience of nearly thirty years in the practical administration of the systems of Public Instruction in the City and State of New York. During the first half of the period, as fellow-laborer with Horace Mann and Henry Barnard, and sitting at the feet of such men as John A. Dix, John C. Spencer, Samuel Young and Christopher Morgan in the State Department, the author could scarcely fail of imbibing the great central truths pertaining to Popular Education and the fundamental principles upon which it should rest. Fourteen years of unremitting labor as Superintendent of the Public Schools of the City of New York have not only served to deepen and strengthen the principles thus acquired, but have suggested many methods of carrying them into successful execution, which could be clearly developed only under such auspices as this great metropolis has afforded.

It is of course quite impracticable in a work of this size to enter into the internal and external details of Public School instruction. I have merely endeavored to point out the foundations and elementary principles which I conceive to be essential to every well-regulated system of Education, and upon which durable and useful superstructures may be erected; illustrating those principles with so much of detail, only, as in my judgment seemed essential to the successful and harmonious operation of these systems throughout the length and breadth of our land.

At the time this work was commenced, the principle of UNIVERSAL and FREE EDUCATION was recognized and practically carried out only in the City of New York and scattered portions of a few of the States of the Union. Now that it has become the watch-word of progress throughout the Republic and in the most enlightened portions of Europe, I flatter myself that any word of encouragement and counsel from one of the humblest pioneers in this great work of the age, may not be altogether unacceptable to those who, by their energy, perseverance and intelligence, have planted the flag of "FREE SCHOOLS" upon the institutions of our National and State governments.

FIRST PRINCIPLES OF POPULAR EDUCATION.

CHAPTER I.

THE PHILOSOPHY OF EDUCATION.

EDUCATION has been properly defined as the development, direction, and culture of the human mind. In its most comprehensive import, it includes the aggregate of all the varied influences brought to bear upon the mind from every source, external or internal, from the cradle to the grave. In a more restricted sense it may be said to consist in that elementary training of the various powers, faculties, and affections of our nature, which shall most effectually fit us for the discharge of all the duties of human life, and enable us adequately to appreciate and faithfully to improve our highest moral and religious nature. The true philosophy of education is therefore to be sought in a careful investigation of our mental and moral faculties, their original destination, the objects and proper ends and aims of our being, and the means by which we may best attain these objects, and accomplish these ends and aims.

It must be obvious to the most superficial thinker, that no system of education can be of any validity, which omits to take into the account, as a primary and indispensable element, the distinctive nature and character of the being to be educated, and the circumstances, both physical and moral, by which he is surrounded. Man is an immortal being, endowed by his Creator with all those faculties, as well of mind as of body, which, properly appreciated and faithfully used, were designed to contribute, in the highest possible degree, to his happiness and well-being here and hereafter. It may not, indeed, be in his power at all times effectually to defend himself from the perpetual incursions of evil in its manifold and myriad shapes: to guard against the innumerable assaults of physical pain to which he is constantly exposed; to avert the approaches of sickness, disease, and death; or to protect himself against the formidable tide of vice and wickedness which unceasingly rolls up its waves at his feet. By the constitution of his physical nature, he is subjected to pain as well as rendered susceptible of pleasure: suffering, no less than enjoyment, is an indispensable portion of his inheritance, and death and the grave, sooner or later, must "have dominion over him;" but he has that within which can enable him to triumph over all the ills of mortality, to convert every affliction into a blessing, to welcome pain and death itself as the harbingers of a new and everlasting life, "where there shall be no more death, neither sorrow nor crying, neither shall there be any more pain." In like manner, by the constitution of his moral nature, evil in some of its multifarious developments must enter as an essential ingredient into his experience, in a world fallen as is ours from its original sinlessness and purity. Vice and wickedness everywhere abound; and no moral or religious atmosphere is so pure as to be wholly free from the pestilential taint of the prevailing plague. But here too "they that are for us are more than they that are against us." We are furnished from the Divine Armory with weapons amply adequate to our protection and defense; and are infallibly assured that our temptations and trials, however many and bitter, shall never exceed our strength or our powers of resistance or endurance; that all the evils of life, all its struggles and conflicts, its alternations of victory and defeat, shall "work together for good," provided only we are true to ourselves, and forget not, amid all our varied experience of human ill, the undying soul and Him from whom it emanates and to whom it shall ascend.

Upon the broad foundations, therefore, of an assured conviction of the immortality of our existence as sentient and intelligent beings, and of the truth of that Christian Revelation which has shed its clear and benignant light upon our path, must we construct the work of education, if we would take account of all the elements which underlie the foundation of character. Without entering upon any of those controverted grounds which have originated and perpetuated distinctive views on the part of numerous sects, all agreeing in the fundamental principles and great leading doctrines of Christianity, we must plant ourselves at once upon those principles and doctrines conceded by all, of every denomination and every sect, who worship and acknowledge one common Creator and Redeemer, and reverently look up to him for guidance and direction in this life, and an immortality of existence in that which is to come, where each shall reap there as he has sown here. Far other and different will be the work of education for a being so circumstanced from that which might well suffice in view of a faith less comprehensive and sublime. If our destiny were restricted to the utmost boundary of our mortal existence, and none of our thoughts or actions, our designs or pursuits, could reach beyond the transitory effects of this present life, many of the noblest and deepest lessons of instruction and wisdom which the Christian pupil must early imbibe and assiduously cherish and obey, would be needless and useless. The ends at which the Christian teacher aims, the motives by which the expanding minds committed to his charge must be guided and governed, the whole course, in short, of intellectual and moral discipline to be pursued in the foundation of the character and the habits, and the direction of the minds, must radically differ. The great truths that we are immortal and responsible beings—that the will of our Creator, in reference to our conduct and our duty, in thought no less than in word and deed, throughout every period of our intelligent existence, has been communicated to us—and that our present and future well-being, in time and throughout eternity, are wholly and inevitably dependent upon the affections we now hourly and daily cultivate and cherish, the actions we now perform, the habits and character we are now engaged in maturing—these convictions, based upon the paramount authority of Divine Revelation, must constitute the corner-stone of every sound and enlightened system of Christian education. The attainment of present pleasure, the gratification of immediate appetite and passion, the acquisition of wealth, of fame, and power, as ultimate ends of our ambition, and the pursuit of knowledge in all its varied and far-reaching shapes, as subsidiary merely to the accomplishment of these objects, or of others terminating with the individual, may all be secured by a process of education in which Christianity, both in the letter and in the spirit, may be ignored; and through this process the intellectual faculties of our nature may be most assiduously and extensively cultivated, and many of the noblest and highest objects of society and of government promoted and accomplished. Such a process, however, falls infinitely short of the demands and requisitions of our higher nature, and leaves its finest issues and its noblest capabilities untouched and undeveloped. Its most prominent and palpable results are before us on every hand: in the prevalence of selfishness in all its diversified forms, infusing its poisonous venom through all the avenues of trade, and tainting with its polluting and soul-hardening influences the holiest charities of social intercourse; in the predominance of the fierce spirit of war and aggression under the most weak and flimsy pretenses of patriotism and public spirit; in the wide-spread corruption and venality which, under color of a noble ambition for the public weal, finds its way into the highest places, and preys, unrebuked and unpunished, upon the very vitals of the State; in the fearful ravages of the lowest and most debasing forms of sensuality, passion and appetite, degrading our nature and contaminating at their fountain-head all those living springs of taste, beauty, and sentiment, which were conferred by the Creator for the most beneficent purposes; and last, though not least, in that miserable perversion of the intellectual and moral faculties of our being, which leads so many, in their judgments of men and things, to reverse the standard of truth and rectitude—to call good evil, and evil good—to crown with the approbation and the favor of community the successful violator of law and order — and to cast every possible obstacle in the path of the upright and conscientious aspirant after honorable distinction and fame. The inevitably downward tendency of such a state of things can never be compensated by the most brilliant discoveries in science, or the highest triumphs of art; and if the car of modern improvement can be impelled only by influences which, in their expansion over the surface of society, are destined to desolate and lay waste the finest flowers of the human heart, surely it were better for the interests both of the community at large, and of the individuals of which it is composed, that the boasted march of civilization should be arrested, and the rushing tide of intellectual conquest turned back. No such necessity, however, exists. Rapid as may be the progress and extensive the conquests of physical and intellectual science, under a system of mental culture which takes comparatively little account of the higher and nobler faculties of man's religious and moral nature, a still wider and more comprehensive sphere awaits the mind's legitimate actions in the full exercise of all its powers, and with the clear consciousness of all its capabilities, responsibilities, and duties, its high origin and noble destination.

Be this as it may, that is unquestionably the only sound basis of an enlightened system of education, which regards its subject as a child of

God, and the heir of immortality—with faculties, affections, and instincts appropriate to this exalted heritage — and capable of attaining the full perfection of its being, and of realizing the wonderful harmonies of its nature only by and through the highest practicable cultivation of each and all these faculties, affections, and emotions, in accordance with the will of its great and beneficent Creator.

CHAPTER II.

THE FAMILY.

REGARDED from the point of view we have thus been led to assume, how vast, how solemn and how responsible is the work of education—how unbounded the field of labor—how full of embarrassments, of difficulties and of obstacles—how incapable of complete and adequate occupation—and how liable to neglect and injudicious culture! At that early and most important period of existence, when the intellectual and moral faculties first dawn upon the horizon of our being, how essential is it that the young should be surrounded by the purest influences, and by an atmosphere of the highest love and wisdom: by instructors prompt to anticipate their struggling and urgent demands for knowledge, and to gratify their restless and ever active curiosity, to store their tender minds with ample and suitable material for thought, wisely to temper the undisciplined luxuriance of their imagination, and to regulate, guide and direct their affections, passions and emotions!

Herein consists the appropriate functions and momentous duties of the Family—that holy institution chartered by the Almighty at the creation of man, and consecrated in all ages by his blessing. In this hallowed circle of love and affection, the child first opens his eyes to the varied phenomena of the external world; and from thenceforth all his senses are tremblingly alive to the countless influences brought to bear upon his rapidly expanding faculties. Evanescent as many of these earliest impressions upon the infant's mind unquestionably are, there can be no doubt that some of the most enduring lessons, some of the most permanent and ineffaceable traits of the future character, are then implanted. A very considerable portion of future well or ill-being may, indeed, spring from physical causes beyond the reach or control of human vigilance or affection, however enlightened and judicious. It is an established fact, and one of most momentous import to all who seek to become parents, that mental and moral, no less than physical characteristics, are not unfrequently transmitted in long succession from one generation to another; and these hereditary tendencies, especially when unfavorable to the permanent welfare of the child, require the most cautious and considerate management. Their existence enters as a most important element into the process of education; and their manifestations, to a greater or less extent, can not fail of exerting a perceptible influence upon the development and formation of character. But aside from this, the daily and hourly incidents of the nursery and family circle—that little world of home within whose sanctuary the energies of the young mind are to unfold themselves, and to receive their earliest and most lasting hue—the conversation, habits, and demeanor of the parents and of those to whose care the child is in any degree confided—the associations with which it is habitually surrounded, the affections and passions manifested, however unconsciously, in its presence, and the entire moral atmosphere in which it is permitted to exist—each and all constitute most powerful and pervading sources of future character and destiny. Those parents, therefore, who from ignorance, inattention, or recklessness neglect those proper sanitary precautions which may serve to strengthen and invigorate the physical health of their offspring, and thereby to shut out a very extensive and fertile source of present suffering and future bodily and mental anguish; or who, absorbed in the pressure of business, or the pursuits of worldly pleasure and ambition, neglect to watch over the gradual development of those young minds committed to their charge; or still more censurably, daily contaminate, by their vicious and profligate example, conversation and habits, the moral nature of their children, are indeed chargeable with a most heinous and irreparable offense, and must be held responsible, in the judgment of mankind and in the estimation of their Creator, for the deplorable consequences which almost invariably follow their improvidence and guilt. If there be a position or a relation in the whole circle of human life, where enlightened and comprehensive knowledge, sound judgment, and an abiding sense of moral and religious duty and responsibility are more indispensable, and the absence of any or either of these characteristics more fraught with fatal consequences than any other, it is that of the parent. However frivolous, ignorant, and unprincipled men and women may claim and exercise the right of "sinning against their own souls" so long as their destiny is unconnected intimately with others, they have *no right* to involve in the guilt of their ignorance or their infamy the dearest interests, for time and eternity, of an innocent and helpless offspring. They have no right to bring into the world beings for whom they are incompetent to provide, physically, intellectually or morally; to give existence to immortal minds, without either the ability or the disposition so to train, cultivate and direct those minds, as to render them the blessings instead of the bane of their possessors, a source of perennial happiness, instead of a turbid and polluted fountain of wretchedness and misery. And the first step of permanent advancement in the true philosophy and science of Education will then only have been taken when the principle shall have been firmly and irrevocably established, as the foundation of social order and individual and general well-being, that Education, in the highest acceptation of the term, shall be universal and free, and that neither the willfully ignorant nor the persistently vicious man or woman shall, under any circumstances, be permitted to contract the relations of marriage, or to give birth to an offspring destined to add to the already sufficiently formidable amount of suffering and misery, physical and moral, with which the world abounds. There can be no hardship, where education is freely dispensed to all, in requiring individuals belonging to either of these classes to place themselves in a condition rightly to estimate and intelligently and conscientiously to perform the duties of any relation they may desire to contract, as an indispensable condition to the enjoyment of its benefits and advantages. There can be no oppression on the part of an enlightened and virtuous community in insisting upon the dispersion of the baleful mists and deadly vapors of ignorance, or the reformation of vicious habits and propensities, on the part of each one of its citizens, as a preliminary to the full participation of the blessings it has to bestow. To the subject of this discipline, no less than to those with whom he is brought into constant contact in the various relations of social life, the requisition insisted upon would be itself the highest blessing; and, with rare exceptions, he himself would gratefully appreciate the boon thus conferred, and cheerfully and promptly embrace the beneficent opportunity thus afforded to attain that mastery and control over his rational and immortal nature which should enable him to become himself the recipient and dispenser of intelligence, happiness and virtue. Why should not, then, the community avail itself of this its rightful authority to prevent the perpetuation of ignorance and vice and misery, by insisting, at all hazards, upon the intellectual and moral culture of each and all its members, and by sternly withholding the enjoyment of its highest, most valuable and most universally sought blessing from those who would only desecrate its hallowed mysteries, and wretchedly pervert its high and holy objects?

From the period when the earliest perceptions and sensations of the external world first dawn upon the infant mind, the process of education may be said to begin. The feelings alternately of pleasure and of pain, at first dim and indistinct, soon connect themselves, intuitively, with the presence or absence of certain persons or things; the assiduous attention and affectionate expression of love and regard manifested by parents, nurses and attendants are early understood and appreciated, and the natural signs of anger, harshness and ill temper speedily perceived and readily interpreted; and in an almost incredibly short time the child adapts and conforms itself to the various circumstances by which it is surrounded; exercises, on however limited and restricted a scale, its capacities of memory, comparison and inference; and makes its first rude essays in the school of practical life. Each succeeding event and sensation of its subsequent experience brings its corresponding lesson, promptly imbibed, and with few and rare exceptions permanently retained, as elements, however inconsiderable in their immediate effects, of the future character. From the incessant and rapid supply of thought and emotion thus furnished to every faculty of the opening nature, many of these germs and elements of subsequent life must necessarily frequently long lie hidden in the deepest recesses of the mind, awaiting the fit occasion and the fit period for their development; and nothing is more common in the ripe experience of the aged, and amid the most importunate pressure of life's varied incidents, than the spontaneous and unexpected reappearance of trains of thought and events long forgotten, but indelibly impressed upon the inner surface of the memory, and it may be of the heart. Who can compute the influences, or measure the effects upon the future destiny, of these innumerable impressions thus made upon the susceptible and retentive mind of childhood? Long years of estrangement from the paths of virtue—of dreary wanderings in the corrupted and corrupting highways of the world—of sad and mournful experience in the vain effort to extract happiness and peace of mind from the "beggarly elements" of ambition, avarice or guilty pleasure, can not effectually blot out, however they may dim, those ineffaceable records of youth and guileless innocence; and often—how often who can know?—they have power, even in the darkest hour of despondency and despair, to rescue the victim of passion and temptation from the deepest gulf of degradation and guilt, and to restore him to rectitude, to virtue, and to God!

The circumstances, therefore, both moral and physical, which surround the child in the infancy of its being, and the influences, favorable or unfavorable, which at that early period are brought to bear upon its susceptible and plastic nature, are of the utmost importance to the future development of its character. They insensibly and gradually, but inevitably, give a direction and a tone to the mental faculties and powers which, whether for good or for evil, can not, without great difficulty and exertion, be subsequently counteracted. They constitute a portion of elementary education far too generally overlooked or neglected; and when so neglected, render the task of the teacher, if faithfully and conscientiously performed, one of exceeding complication and embarrassment. Habits have been contracted and dispositions formed and nourished which can be eradicated only with great labor and long discipline; and elements of character suffered to germinate which, in spite of every effort for their repression, may be destined in after years fatally to overshadow the most promising fruits of intellectual and moral culture, and to exert a most disastrous influence upon the future destiny and life. An enlightened knowledge of the elementary principles and most important conclusions of physiological science, coupled with the ability and the disposition firmly, systematically and habitually to apply that knowledge and those principles, with a judicious reference to constitutional peculiarities and circumstances; habitual control of the temper and the passions; the most exemplary, moral and religious deportment, in all the varied relations of life; a cultivated and refined taste; and the uniform indulgence of kindly and affectionate dispositions, combined with a no less uniform and invariable repression of vicious propensities and habits in their earliest bud; these qualifications and acquirements on the part as well of parents as of teachers, accompanied by a cheerful, kindly and elevating social atmosphere, and the innumerable sources of innocent and healthful pleasure which nature has so bountifully and benignantly spread out to every uncorrupted sense, will constitute the surest and most reliable foundation for that generous culture of the intellect and the heart which is alone worthy the name of Education.

CHAPTER III.

PUBLIC INSTRUCTION.

THE foundations of education and of character having thus been laid in the domestic circle, the child is, usually at an early period, committed to the charge of the elementary teacher. The important functions thus delegated should, undoubtedly, for as long a time as may be in any degree practicable, continue to be discharged by the parents themselves, or at all events under their immediate supervision and direction in the familiar sanctuary of home. If, however, the school is what it should be, the teacher properly qualified, both intellectually and morally, for the discharge of the high duties devolving upon him, and the surrounding influences of the school-room in all respects unobjectionable, the transfer of the pupil from the circumscribed sphere to which he has hitherto been restricted to a new and more enlarged field of action and of effort, can scarcely prove otherwise than beneficial. And this leads us at once to the consideration of the vitally important subject of PUBLIC INSTRUCTION: a subject of the deepest interest alike to governments, to communities and to individuals.

In what way, by what means, and to what extent the State, in its political capacity, may promote the interests and subserve the objects of popular education—what are the duties and responsibilities incumbent upon the great body of the people, in reference to the intellectual and moral culture of the future citizens of the commonwealth — and how those duties may most effectually be performed, and those responsibilities adequately met, are problems which have long engaged the attention and occupied the efforts of the statesman and philanthropist, but hitherto without results at all corresponding to the magnitude of the interests at stake. By some it has been maintained that every civilized community possesses the power and the right to withdraw the child wholly from the parent, and to place him under the exclusive guardianship and care of instructors named by and responsible only to the State; while others have denied both the expediency and the right of interference on the part of the government, to any extent whatever, in the education of the young. These, however, are extreme views on both sides, and like all other extreme views upon subjects of practical importance in the conduct of human life, are to be received with great caution, if not entirely rejected and discountenanced. The right of the State to take cognizance of the education of its future citizens, if it be conceded to exist, must, undoubtedly, be exercised in subordination to, or concurrently with, the paramount right of its component members to the unrestricted enjoyment of all those social, domestic, and individual privileges for which governments and society itself exist; and any regulation which, under pretenses even of a greater ultimate good, should undertake to contravene this fundamental principle would, it is conceived, be not only impolitic, but unjust and oppressive. On the other hand, to deny to the body-politic any jurisdiction whatever over the mental and moral culture of the youth of the State, and to exclude from the legitimate domain of legislation every thing pertaining to the work of education, would be effectually to neutralize the influence of every other salutary agency in the machinery of human government, and to render the progress of improvement absolutely impossible. The power to punish the criminal offender would seem not more certainly and unquestionably an attribute of all governments, than that of restraining and preventing the commission of the crime itself, whenever and wherever such restraint and prevention may be practicable and attainable: and the same fundamental laws which are confessedly competent, in the prosecution of the great objects for which they are instituted, to interfere with the liberty and even to take the life of the transgressor and the felon, are surely no less competent to prescribe and to adopt those means of prevention which may avert the necessity of such punishment, and thereby free the community from all those repulsive and demoralizing concomitants which are found almost invariably to follow in its train. The obligation and the duty of the State to provide a proper asylum and a comfortable support for the indigent and the helpless is generally admitted; its *right* to do so unquestioned by any. Is it, then, to be presumed that no power exists in the legislative department of the government to adopt such prudential measures as observation and experience may from time to time suggest, for the diminution of those physical and moral evils, which lie at the root of pauperism and mendicity? A supposition so strikingly at variance with every dictate of sound wisdom and practical morality, is scarcely to be tolerated by any mind at all conversant with the fundamental principles of an enlightened political economy.

The concurrent testimony of the ablest and most experienced educators of our own and other lands affords the most conclusive assurances that under a well-administered and efficient system of universal education, "*ninety-nine out of every hundred*, even of the generation first submitted to the experiment, may be rendered honest dealers, conscientious jurors, true witnesses, incorruptible voters or magistrates, good parents, good neighbors, good members of society, temperate, industrious and frugal, conscientious in all their dealings, prompt to pity and instruct ignorance, public-spirited, philanthropic, and observers of all things sacred." Has then the State, in its corporate capacity, no interest in this great work—no power to help it on—no aid to render it—no encouragement, sympathy, or co-operation to bestow upon it? It has been fully and repeatedly demonstrated by scientific and practical men, that the aggregate amount of industry in any community may be immensely increased by means of general and specific intellectual culture; that in any given pursuit, trade, or occupation, the individual of most varied information and accurate knowledge possesses decided advantages in the accumulation and rational enjoyment of wealth over all competitors less favored in this regard; and that the various avenues leading to mercantile, manufacturing, or agricultural success, may be far more profitably occupied by the educated, than by the ignorant or the superficial. Has the State, as such, no concern in this? Has it no functions by means of which it can encourage and reward individual or associated enterprise or exertion — can repress and discourage indolence and sloth—can remove the pressure of poverty—expand the operations of agriculture, manufactures, and commerce, and build the superstructure of national greatness upon the desirable foundations of an enlightened and well-directed industry?

Such has not been the construction hitherto put upon the high objects of government and legislation by the great statesmen and profound politicians of our own or other lands. From whence, it may be inquired, do we derive the very existence of property? what gives to it its value? what protects, preserves, and defends it against violence, subtlety, fraud, and craft? and what enables its possessor to enjoy and to use it with safety and profit? Is it not the power and the influence of a paternal government, securing the prevalence of good order throughout the community, establishing and maintaining just laws, affording adequate remedies for their violation, and watching over the welfare and safety of the humblest equally with the highest citizen of the commonwealth?

And has not the general diffusion of sound knowledge, the inculcation of pure morality, the formation of virtuous habits, the presence and operation of a pervading sentiment of integrity, an undeniable tendency to render the possession and enjoyment of property more secure, more valuable and certain? Do they not immeasurably enhance its worth, encourage its acquisition, and ensure its profits? Surely we have only to contrast our own privileges in this respect with that general insecurity which prevails in the semi-civilized or barbarous nations of the Old World, and which uniformly accompanies the prevalence of ignorance and moral degradation, to be convinced of these facts. And is it not within the personal experience of most business men, that the pecuniary value of real estate, especially when thrown into market, is in a very great degree affected, favorably or adversely, by the presence or absence of an enlightened, orderly, and law-abiding neighborhood? Should not then the aggregate wealth of the State be applied, to such an extent as may be necessary, to furnish an ample fund, the avails of which are to be thus expended in providing every citizen a sure guaranty for the undisturbed enjoyment of his home, his possessions, and his personal rights?

If then it be true that the general and unrestricted diffusion of knowledge has a direct and necessary tendency to prevent the commission of crime, by removing all inducements to evil courses, and by substituting in their stead the operation of motives leading to a diametrically opposite result—if it be true that the prevalence of sound and enlightened views of intellectual and moral culture, and the general reduction of these views to practice, would, in all human probability, result in the speedy extinction of mendicity, or would at all events restrict it to cases of rare occurrence, and such as are beyond the reach of ordinary remedies—and if all history, observation, and experience concur in the principle that the elevation, the prosperity and advancement of individuals, of communities and of nations in physical and material no less than in mental and moral well-being, are uniformly in a direct ratio to their attainments in knowledge and their progress in virtue—the inference would seem to be irresistible that the first, the most sacred duty of a Christian State, is adequately to provide for the proper education of all its citizens. Individual effort in this direction, however judiciously applied and energetically prosecuted, will almost inevitably be found incompetent to the attainment of the object in view; and while through the penury and inability of some, the indifference of more, and the open hostility of others, the progress made by the most devoted friends of education might be neutralized and their exertions rendered unavailing, is it for a moment to be admitted that the potent arm of the State is so shortened and paralyzed that it can not interpose to strengthen the feeble, to give confidence to the timid and wavering, and to remove the numerous and formidable obstacles thrown in the path of improvement by the vicious, the idle, and the indifferent? Such a supposition is wholly at variance with every sound principle of government and legislation.

We regard it, therefore, as imperative upon the State, that elementary instruction should be freely and equally dispensed to all, in institutions recognized, sanctioned, and sustained by itself, open at all times to the rich and to the poor—"without money and without price"—that this instruction should be, in all cases, adequate to the communication of that degree of knowledge, at least, which shall enable its recipient intelligently and efficiently to perform all those duties which, in the ordinary course of human events, and the intercourse of society, may devolve upon him, and to attain such farther and higher acquirements as his ambition or inclination may require; and that by the proper preparation of a suitable number of teachers, thoroughly conversant with their profession, and skilled in all its practical details, an adequate inducement may be presented to the community at large to avail itself of their services, and to bring within the school thus established every child of suitable age to be benefited by their instruction and discipline. We claim that the right of every child in the State to such an education as shall be adequate to the proper discharge of the obligations and responsibilities incident to human life, should be distinctly recognized and efficiently guaranteed by the supreme power of the State, and that the means of securing such an education should be provided by an equal and just assessment upon its aggregate wealth. With especial reference to our country and its institutions, we insist that in a republican form of government, where all political power emanates, directly or indirectly, from the people themselves, general education is absolutely indispensable, and of vital and paramount importance; that, from the earliest period of our existence as a people, this principle has been recognized and acted upon by those communities where the greatest moral, social, and political advancement has been made; that it has taken root and flourished wherever the great body of the people have tested its advantages and afforded it a fair scope for developing its capabilities; and that wherever it has been introduced and obtained a firm foothold, it has never been abandoned. We allege that upon the general prevalence of intelligence and virtue, of sound science and uncorrupted morality, not only the happiness and welfare of each individual of the community, but the very foundations of society and government, essentially depend; that the wealth and resources of the community can in no mode be so profitably and advantageously invested, even in a merely pecuniary point of view, than by the promotion and general diffusion of useful knowledge; and that every dollar thus contributed to the mental and moral culture of the youth of the State, at that important period when the rudiments of character are in process of formation, is an actual saving of hundreds of thousands, which, in the absence or neglect of such culture, must be lavished within a few brief years in the conviction and punishment of crime, or the support of mendicants and paupers. Finally, we insist that while the State, in its civil and political capacity, undoubtedly possesses the power of repressing every infraction of its laws and ordinances, and of imposing upon the whole body of its citizens an annual tax for defraying the enormous expenditure incident to the administration of criminal justice, it as undoubtedly possesses the power of *prevention*, in the provision of early and ample facilities for the education and instruction of its future citizens, thereby removing every inducement and inclination to vice and crime, and substituting in their stead nobler and higher aims, purer aspirations, and wiser and better motives of action; and that the obvious dictates of common policy, no less than of a sound and enlightened political economy, point to the expediency and salutary efficacy of such ample provision for the *education* and *instruction* of the rising generation as shall preclude the necessity of an immensely greater outlay for their future *punishment* and *support.*

These are some of the advantages and blessings which the advocates of Universal Education, through a system of schools open and free to all, supported and liberally endowed by the government of the State itself, propose to secure: the diminution of vice and crime by the effectual removal of every inducement to their perpetration, and by the early formation of habits and dispositions at variance with their existence; the prevention of pauperism and mendicity by the bestowment of the power and the will to accomplish all the necessary objects of human existence; and the general prevalence of integrity, humanity, benevolence, industry, and public and private morality by the timely and assiduous inculcation of all those pure and elevating principles which refine and ennoble our common nature. The future welfare and prosperity of each individual will thus become indissolubly associated with those of every other, in the bonds of one common interest; fully aware that the sole security for the undisturbed enjoyment and quiet possession of the property each may accumulate or obtain is to be found in the integrity, intelligence and virtue of the surrounding community, and that the every existence and perpetuation of the government under which these blessings are to be enjoyed, these rights and immunities secured and obtained, are dependent upon an enlightened and uncorrupted public sentiment.

CHAPTER IV.

THE SCHOOL—ELEMENTARY INSTRUCTION.

THE education of the senses, the discipline of the affections and passions, and the formation of the habits, constitute the earliest task of the elementary teacher. Before the intellect can perform the various processes of comparison, analysis, thought, reason and imagination, it must be furnished with the materials upon which to exercise its powers; and while the disposition is yet docile, the passions undeveloped, and the will unbiased, that direction should be given to the plastic energies of the moral nature which will most effectually preserve it from the evil tendencies to which it is destined to be exposed, and those habits superinduced which will serve as ever present and potent auxiliaries to a uniform course of virtue in after life. This portion of education, as it is by far the most important, and most decisive of the future character, so it should commence under the paternal guidance with the earliest dawn of consciousness, and be unintermittingly prosecuted through every subsequent stage of progress.

The first impressions of childhood—its earliest associations when life is new and existence itself one continued source of pleasure and enjoyment—are, as is well known, the most lasting and durable. Each successive acquisition affords intense delight and fixes itself permanently in the memory. Each exertion of the incipient powers, each sensation of the expanding being, each involuntary emotion and affection excited into activity by the passing scenes and events of the narrow circle into which the experience of the young learner is compressed, becomes the germ of future action and character. How important then that no element of falsehood and deception should be interposed to obscure the dawning conceptions, that no unnecessary obstacles should be thrown in the path of knowledge, and above all, that no exhibition of angry passions or of evil and vicious habits should be permitted to cast its withering blight upon the tender and susceptible heart!

Early, however, as is the period, in the generality of instances, when the course of instruction is commenced in the school, the teacher finds much of error to be unlearned—many false and inaccurate conceptions to be corrected—many evil passions to be repressed—many injurious habits to be eradicated—many new principles to be implanted, cherished and cultivated. The associations of the school-room are well calculated to foster and promote these important objects. The strict regard to discipline — the uniform order, regularity and system which prevail — the rigid enforcement of obedience, punctuality, neatness and decorum—the periodical alternations of study and relaxation—the varied exercises of the class-room—all serve to impress upon the pupil's mind the most salutary and beneficial lessons, and lead him imperceptibly to regard himself as a constituent portion of the little community to which he has become attached—interested in its welfare as something distinct from his own individual personality—a participant in its benefits and enjoyments—responsible to others for his conduct and attainments—and while subjected to the wholesome restraints of a necessary discipline, exposed to the good or ill opinion of his associates, the approbation or censure of all who take an interest in his welfare, and the scrutinizing regard of the public authorities. That desire for knowledge, inherent in every well-constituted mind — that restless, insatiable curiosity and inquisitiveness peculiar to childhood—find their gratification at each successive step of progress, while excited to fresh explorations in the wide domain of science, knowledge soon becomes desirable for its own sake — is its own exceeding great reward. The mind of the learner grows more and more interested as it gradually opens to the objects and uses of the lessons daily communicated, and begins to explore, by the aid of the new resources placed at its command, the wonders and beauties of the external universe.

Nature assumes a new and deeply interesting aspect, as the flower, the leaf and the grass, the vegetable, the plant and the mineral are analyzed and decomposed—their structure, functions, objects, uses, means and ends pointed out — their relations to man explained—their position in the great scheme of creative wisdom and beneficence illustrated and defined—their origin and history rendered "familiar as household words," and all those associations which connect them with the daily pursuits and highest welfare of mankind brought to bear, through those familiar illustrations which the well-informed teacher can render so attractive and instructive. Those elementary branches of study usually so irksome and so tedious under the guidance of the mere pedagogue, become invested with the deepest interest, and clothed with the most captivating charms, when informed with life and animation by the potent wand of the true teacher. The acquisition of the alphabet and its combination into words and syllables become a labor of love, when their connection with the inexhaustible treasures of learning and science through the medium of books is fully explained and comprehended; and the task involved in the reading-lesson is forgotten in the absorbing interest of the subject. Orthography and grammar, when regarded as the indispensable accompaniments of a graceful and accurate expression, are readily and easily mastered; geography, when combined with and illustrated by history, and a clear, simple and intelligible exposition of the form, structure, movements, and position of the planet on which we live, assumes at once a lively interest; and even the abstruse combinations of arithmetic are found to possess a fascinating charm the moment its complicated researches are discovered to have an intrinsic and practical value, and an application to the most important and interesting pursuits of life.

The foundations and elementary principles of the highest mathematics, of astronomy, natural philosophy, chemistry and geology, may in this attractive manner be advantageously and firmly laid in the primary school. By familiar expositions, conversation and simple illustrations, a spirit of animated inquiry and research is elicited on the part of the least advanced pupils, which leads insensibly to farther and more complete investigation, and excites an interest in the youthful mind which can not be repressed. The spirit of inquiry and research can not be too diligently encouraged and fostered on the part of parents and teachers. It affords a source of pleasurable occupation to the child—diverts its mind from frivolous pursuits—prevents it from yielding up its faculties and powers to indolence and sloth—secures it against the numerous temptations to vicious pursuits and indulgences, and prepares it for those nobler and higher efforts which lead to greatness and to fame. It imbues the intellect with valuable and practical ideas, while its invariable tendency is to enlarge the affections and to strengthen and invigorate the moral powers, by directing and fastening the attention upon the wonderful and beautiful manifestations in the world, both of matter and of mind, of the infinite and all-wise Creator. I know of no more salutary and profitable mental and moral discipline which can be bestowed upon the child on its first introduction into our institutions of elementary instruction, and during the entire period of its continuance there, than those unpretending and simple, but deeply interesting and instructive lessons on the objects which surround us in the external universe, the uses they respectively subserve in the economy of nature, their adaptations to the varied pursuits of industry and science and the arts of life, the laws which they obey, their origin and history, and their mutual interdependence and connection. For want of this early and continued discipline, how many of our ripest scholars and most eminent men still remain profoundly ignorant of many of those fundamental laws and principles which regulate and preside over the development of the most important phenomena of the planet on which they exist! How many among our population, of all classes and grades, experience numerous and serious misfortunes, commit grievous practical errors, and suffer constant embarrassment and inconvenience! How much of energy and talent and tact, which rightly directed and skillfully applied might have accomplished great and beneficent results, is wasted, perverted and misapplied; and how lamentably and seriously has the progress of true knowledge among the mass of mankind been retarded by the prevalence of erroneous views and the adoption of false and unsound principles of action!

CHAPTER V.

INTELLECTUAL CULTURE.

THE most ample provision should be made in every enlightened system of education for the development and culture of *all* the faculties, intellectual and moral, of the mind. With this view, an adequate and comprehensive knowledge of those faculties, their mode of operation, the legitimate sphere of their action, and of their distinctive peculiarities, is indispensable. Without attempting the impracticable task of sounding the depths of mental and moral philosophy so clearly expounded by the ablest metaphysicians and divines of ancient and modern times, the prominent results of these investigations, as confirmed and established by the observation and experience of successive ages, may be briefly adverted to.

It is an incontrovertible principle of a sound philosophy of the human mind, that for every faculty, affection and emotion of our complex nature, an appropriate and legitimate field of action and exertion has been prepared; and that within this range, all its operations are attended with pleasure, with improvement and benefit. Each of these faculties, affections and emotions, is, however, liable to perversion and abuse: and whenever through ignorance, recklessness or design, the beneficent law of its functions is transcended, the inevitable and invariable consequence of such departure is sooner or later experienced in positive suffering and misery, physical or moral, and to an extent corresponding with the importance of the fundamental law or principle which has thus been violated. Every institution of the Creator throughout the vast amplitude of his manifestations, and especially in the domain of the human mind, is clearly indicative of the highest wisdom, and most unbounded love; and in all the operations of his hands no element of evil exists except through the transgression of those laws which he has ordained for the highest happiness and well-being of his creatures.

The power of transgression—the ability freely, and without other restraint than the knowledge of his will and of our duty, the dictates of conscience, and of the voice of God within our soul—to conform to the law of our being, in accordance with the clear injunctions of that inward monitor enthroned in every breast, and with the corresponding oracles of Divine Truth communicated in the Holy Scriptures, or to depart from that law, trample upon these injunctions, and disregard these high oracles—this power and ability are essential and necessary concomitants of humanity—by which alone we attain to the proper dignity of our nature, and without which we sink to the level of the beasts that perish.

Among the various faculties of the human mind, *the desire of knowledge* seems to be earliest developed. To this end the perceptions and sensitive powers—those which take cognizance of the phenomena of the external world and of the feelings and emotions of the sentient nature within, are conferred, and find a wide and diversified scope of action, constantly enlarging and expanding with the experience of each individual. At first these perceptions and emotions are vague, indistinct and unintelligible. By imperceptible degrees, however, they become more clear and definite, and capable of being sharply discriminated and referred to their appropriate classes in the rapid succession of events. One field after another of knowledge is appropriated, and to a greater or less extent mentally digested and arranged; and in comparatively a very brief period, a vast amount of valuable information, more or less accurate and reliable, is accumulated for future use. This process is one of exceeding interest and importance; and it is specially incumbent upon parents and teachers not only to encourage and promote its exercise on all suitable occasions, but to render its results practical and useful in the highest possible degree, with reference to all the future contingencies of life, and to the growth and comprehensiveness of the intellectual and moral power.

The natural and urgent curiosity of the young inquirer should never be repressed and seldom diverted; and full, *specific*, and accurate information should be communicated on all topics within the compass of the tender understanding. Large and frequent excursions should be made into the boundless domains of Nature in all her wonderful and beautiful manifestations, and the eager and docile attention of the deeply-interested learner directed into those attractive channels of investigation and knowledge which are capable of yielding the most valuable and profitable results for subsequent thought and improvement. The active and retentive energies of the youthful intellect will rapidly absorb and assimilate the mental food thus placed within its reach, and its faculties, fresh and unwearied, will store up in the receptacles of the unburdened memory, ample supplies for its future aliment. The value of early, general and accurate knowledge thus agreeably and pleasurably obtained, can scarcely be too highly estimated. It affords not only a delightful, innocent and ever accessible source of occupation to the restless energies, both physical and mental, of the young, but an inexhaustible well-spring of intellectual and moral truth and beauty, which will diffuse its refreshing waters over the entire surface of subsequent life. Confused, imperfect, and inaccurate conceptions, no less than blank ignorance or gross error, involve innumerable elements of misfortune and error.

It has been observed, not without a strong foundation in the experience of individuals and communities, that ignorance is itself the chief and prolific source of error and of guilt; that with clear perceptions of truth, neither the understanding nor the reason could be essentially led astray, nor the higher moral and religious faculties perverted, and that an early, full and enlightened comprehension of the elementary principles and details of science, of the manifestations and laws of the various phenomena of the external world, could not fail gradually but surely to extirpate the numerous and baleful seeds of human error and consequent suffering. Certain it is, that a very large proportion of the ills of life, physical as well as moral, are fairly attributable to the absence of sound and accurate knowledge; to a failure or inability to comprehend the great laws of the universe of matter and of mind, and the invariable relations they sustain to each other and to the permanent well-being of the race; to the want of an early familiarity with the fundamental principles of scientific inquiry and research, and to the unjustifiable neglect, on the part of those to whom the education of the young is confided, to cultivate, cherish, and direct that innate and irrepressible spirit of curiosity and that ardent desire for knowledge which is the universal characteristic of the youthful mind. Early impressions, whether true or false, are of unyielding tenacity. They incorporate themselves permanently into the character, and become constituent portions of the principles which regulate and determine the whole of future life; and by their expansion and diffusion, a tone and an impulse are given to the whole body, politic and social. The interests of true wisdom and virtue may be thus extensively promoted and advanced, or the dominions of error and of vice increased, strengthened and perpetuated, by the true or false direction given to the earliest aspirations and strongest impulses of the expanding intellect.

The desire of knowledge is, in its primary manifestations, purely an intellectual faculty, embracing in its scope the entire phenomena of the visible universe, irrespective of their practical value or the various uses to which they may be applied. The special function of the teacher consists in the systematic classification and proper arrangement of this knowledge in such a form as to render it available for future thought and action. To this end, in addition to the ordinary elementary branches of instruction, the science of natural history in all its varieties, of natural philosophy, physiology, the higher mathematics, astronomy, chemistry and geology, with their kindred pursuits, accompanied by ample illustrations and experiments, should engage the early and assiduous attention of the pupil. Ancient and modern history should be thoroughly mastered, and a due proportion of time devoted to the acquisition of the languages. No department of useful knowledge should be neglected, even though its results should have no direct bearing upon the future pursuits of the student. The portion of time, however, and the degree of attention to be bestowed upon each, should have reference to the circumstances and condition of the individual, to the peculiar profession, trade, or occupation for which he may be designed, to his predominant taste or genius, and to the general characteristics of the age and the community in which his lot has been cast. The acquisition of knowledge in all its branches, however thorough and general, and indispensable as it is to all subsequent progress, is the foundation only of the work of education —the process by which the *materials* for future culture and improvement are supplied, and the store-house of the mind furnished with adequate instruments for its important operations.

The higher faculties of reason, judgment and imagination—the powers of combination, comparison and discrimination—next demand our attention, and require the most judicious and careful development. Facts being supplied from every attainable source, elementary principles acquired and established, and the vast panorama of nature and art spread out before our view, the enlargement and expansion of the intellectual domain by means of thought, reflection, reason and fancy, become the congenial occupation of the more advanced mind. The various uses, objects, and ends of the knowledge which has been acquired, its capacity of subserving the practical pursuits of life, the benefit and interest of individuals and communities, and the advancement and promotion of the moral and religious nature; the mode in which those uses, objects and ends may most effectually be accomplished, and the practicability of still farther and higher excursions into the realms of thought and imagination—all these sources of future usefulness should be systematically opened and explained.

While, however, in every well-regulated system of education, ample provision should be made for the highest possible cultivation of each and all these faculties, careful discrimination is necessary in individual instances, with reference to the earlier or later development of the several intellectual powers, the prevailing bias of mind, and the peculiar circumstances and situation of each. The infinite diversity in these and other equally important respects, so abundantly manifest in the capacities, inclinations, and conditions of different individuals, palpably requires the most vigilant attention and the most judicious guidance on the part of the teacher. Every faculty of the human mind should undoubtedly be developed and cultivated; each, however, in its appropriate season, and conformably to its relation and connection with all the others, and to the peculiar idiosyncrasy of the possessor; and a wise and constant reference should be had to his actual position in life, and probable future pursuits and sphere of action. From the well-known and universally conceded influence of physical causes, hereditary tendencies, and surrounding circumstances, the intellectual powers of one individual may be prematurely and rapidly developed, while those of another may, to a very great extent, remain long in abeyance and inaction. One manifests at a very early period an insatiable thirst for knowledge, and an ability to grasp and to retain all the great results of literature and science, with a due appreciation of their relative importance and value, while another may long vegetate in utter indifference to their claims, or without comprehending any thing beyond the groveling and contracted sphere of his animal existence. To the finer issues of the mental constitution of the one, all nature presents one vast theatre of harmony, richness and beauty, and his ears are open to the ravishing melody of those great master spirits of poetry, philosophy and eloquence, who in every age and in every clime have discoursed of its varied manifestations, and of the powers, faculties, and destination of humanity; while to the obtuse and blunted senses of the other, all these inexhaustible sources of pleasure and improvement are utterly uncongenial and unknown. For one mind, the arts of painting, statuary, music, or machinery possess an engrossing and irresistible attraction; for another, the more practical pursuits of statesmanship, legislation and political economy; for another, literature and science, the professions of law, medicine or divinity, or some of the numerous avocations of business or pleasure which minister to the profit, advantage, or temporal happiness of those engaged in their pursuit.

All these peculiarities and circumstances, affecting, as they necessarily must, the entire intellectual and moral constitution, and exerting a most important influence upon the formation of the future character, are carefully and judiciously to be taken into the account, and made the basis of the mental culture. When one or more faculties are disproportionately developed, to such an extent as clearly to indicate a predominant and overshadowing influence over others, every effort should be made to restore, as far as may be practicable, the equilibrium of the mental powers, not so much by repressing the manifestations or restricting the exercise of the former, as by assiduously cultivating and bringing forward the latter.

Every attempt, openly or covertly, by authority or persuasion, to restrain or subdue the powerful tendencies of a mind thus constituted toward the legitimate objects of its preference, will be found either utterly futile or eminently, and it may be permanently, disastrous in its results. Except in cases where positive evil or injury may reasonably be anticipated from an unrestrained indulgence in the master-passion of the intellect, the only safe counteracting agency is conceived to lie in a judicious and systematic *diversion* of the attention to other mental exercises and pursuits, and by investing these with the greatest possible attractions. The brilliant hues of the imagination and fancy may thus advantageously be thrown over the less congenial and more practical pursuits of the intellect, elevating these to a more commanding height, and softening and modifying those to a nearer conformity to the palpable realities of every-day life. The exactness, precision, and perfect symmetry of mathematical demonstration, may profitably be brought to bear upon the excessive tendency of the imaginative powers to an unrestrained and luxuriant development, and each faculty of the mind in its turn allowed to strengthen, modify, or restrain the action of every other in strict accordance with those higher principles and laws which should preside over all. The entire and absorbing devotion of the intellect and the heart to one engrossing passion or pursuit, and the concentration of all the physical and mental energies upon that idol of the affection, however conducive to the progress and perfection of particular sciences, arts, or industrial avocations, and however contributing to the formation and maturity of strongly marked character and originality, are manifestly unfavorable to that equable and healthy growth of mental and moral character which alone can enable the individual to fulfill his whole duty to himself, to the community of which he is a member, and to his Creator.

CHAPTER VI.

SYSTEMS OF INSTRUCTION.

THAT system of instruction is the soundest and best which, in the shortest period of time, most fully and completely develops the mental faculties equably, harmoniously, and in accordance with the practical functions required of each, in the intercourse with the world. The mere communication of knowledge, of whatever kind, is not instruction. The ability and the disposition to receive, to understand, and to profit by it, must exist. The attention must be awakened; an interest in the subject under consideration must be excited; elementary principles and habits of thought must be formed; and that persevering industry which refuses to abandon any investigation until its purport is thoroughly comprehended, must be cultivated. Clearness of conception and a systematic process of instruction are also most important, if not indispensable requisites to the attainment of solid instruction in any and every department of scientific research.

It is incumbent, therefore, upon the teacher, in the outset of his labors, so to discipline and prepare the minds of his pupils as to enable them efficiently to co-operate with him in the work of instruction. They must be thrown to as great an extent as possible upon their own intellectual resources. They must be taught not only the rudiments and first principles of knowledge, but *how to think*, and how to obtain knowledge for themselves. They must be made acquainted with the powers, faculties, and capabilities of their own minds, and accustomed at the earliest practicable period to exert their own energies of thought and reason, of discrimination and deduction. Self-reliance and the power of self-instruction should be inculcated and conferred: and nothing superficial, nothing incapable of clear and satisfactory elucidation from their own intellectual stores, should be permitted to pass current for genuine knowledge.

Perhaps the most important preliminary to a systematic course of instruction consists in a proper classification of pupils, with reference not merely to their respective attainments, but to their general capacities and peculiar genius and talents. This, in the majority of instances, will require considerable time, close observation, and the exercise of nice discrimination on the part of the teacher. It not unfrequently happens that in the examination of some of the more advanced classes in our schools, the chief burden falls upon a very few who exhibit a remarkable degree of ability, while a majority of their associates are correspondingly deficient. This indicates an erroneous classification, and is productive of the most injurious consequences to the future progress of those pupils who have thus been left behind. A comparison of their own attainments with those of their associates induces discouragement and despondency. The inability to sustain themselves in the position assigned them by their instructors, and the failure to meet the expectations of their teachers and friends, paralyze their ambition and relax their exertions, and serious injustice is done to their real acquirements and merits. They feel that in their proper position they could have accomplished all that was required of them; that although deficient in those acquisitions for which their companions have been awarded the prize of excellence, their deficiency was attributable to no lack of industry or of effort on their part, but to an original inequality of attainment or of endowment which, while it may have retarded their progress, and placed them in a false position with reference to their associates, in reality afforded no true standard of their merit—no criterion of their advancement. Or, it may happen, that in some other department of science or branch of study, more congenial to their taste or better adapted to their peculiar powers and faculties, they would have taken their station in the front ranks of excellence and superiority. It should, therefore, be the aim of the teacher thoroughly to acquaint himself, at the earliest practicable period, with the peculiar tendencies, powers, and capacities of each individual mind subjected to his discipline, and so to arrange his classes as to afford each a full and fair opportunity for the just and equal development of its faculties. The pupil, who in one branch may be deemed adequate to compete with the most advanced minds of an advanced class, in another may find his level in the lowest, and in others still occupy a suitable and advantageous position in some of the various intermediate grades.

Great care should be taken to bring the chief burden of instruction to bear upon those branches of learning in which the pupil is most deficient, and for which he exhibits the least aptitude or inclination. In those departments to which his taste and genius most strongly direct him, he will require but a slight and occasional stimulus. Nothing is more fatal to all true progress than that prevailing system of *hot-bed cultivation*, which, for purposes of ostentation and display, concentrates all its energies upon those powers in which the pupil manifests precocious and extraordinary endowments, to the utter or comparative neglect of others equally essential to his success in life, and to the harmonious structure of his character. Premature and excessive manifestations of peculiar faculties, instead of being thus encouraged and stimulated, should rather be repressed, and at all events counteracted in their morbid development by the most diligent culture of other powers. The brilliant triumphs of early and extraordinary genius, restricted to its own peculiar sphere, and excited by injudicious applause and unrepressed admiration, are but too frequently the precursors of lasting bitterness and disappointment. All history and experience demonstrate their danger, and lift up a solemn voice of warning against their fatal and disastrous tendency. Genius, in whatever form of honorable and laudable ambition it may be manifested, is a glorious and a divine gift — a gift which should be cherished, cultivated, and applied to the highest and noblest purposes of life. But it should neither be idolized nor perverted from its true mission by the neglect of other faculties essential to its growth and indispensable to its healthy development. Let it never be forgotten that where much is given, there much will be required — that the individual upon whom has been conferred the noblest intellectual power, holds it in trust for the human race, and is responsible for its faithful exercise to his Creator and to his fellow-men; that he can not with impunity waste his talent, or neglect its proper cultivation; and that while he sounds the deepest and highest notes of eloquence or of poetry, or pours forth the inexhaustible stores of metaphysical lore, or solves the profoundest problems of mathematical science, or executes the most skillful combination of art, he may not trample upon the obligations of our common humanity — he may not disregard the duties incumbent upon him as a man and a Christian—he may not demand an exemption from those practical claims which society requires—and he may not use those god-like powers which elevate him above the mass of his brethren to their injury or degradation. An equable cultivation of all the intellectual and moral faculties to such an extent as to secure the ready and effective use of each, the entire command and control of all, and that just balance which prevents the undue ascendancy or usurpation of any—constitutes the only true theory of education in its application not only to the ordinary class of minds, but especially to those of more ethereal mould—the children of genius and the heirs of fame.

Instruction should be communicated, as far as possible, *suggestively*, instead of dogmatically. The pupil should be aided no farther than is absolutely requisite to enable him to obtain the necessary insight into the subject-matter of his inquiries. He should be thrown upon his own resources, and prompted only when they fail him. Principles should be early and assiduously inculcated, and thoroughly illustrated and applied; and then the pupil should be left to carry them out in all their details, and to extend their application as widely as he may desire. No substantial or useful progress can be made where this process is reversed—where the various operations of science are mechanically performed with no just conception of the principles involved—where the pupil gives himself up to the dictation of the teacher or of the text-book, and is content with the ability, parrot-like, to repeat the instructions of the former, and reproduce the lesson of the latter. The mind must put forth its own powers, plume its own wings, and soar upon the strength of its own pinions if it would ascend to those clear regions of knowledge and power which extend far beyond the mists and exhalations of error and ignorance. What the age in which we live most imperatively requires is men and women of earnest, comprehensive, clear minds —unfettered by prejudice, bigotry, and delusion —prompt to discern the true aspect of things—ready to welcome and embrace truth, in whatsoever guise she may present herself, but eagle-eyed in detecting falsehood and sophistry in whatever mask arrayed, or under whatever pretense attempted to be imposed upon mankind; men and women capable of original thinking — of sound discrimination — of high and noble views — of cultivated intellects and disciplined affections — thoroughly familiar with the history of their race — appreciating and venerating all that the past has transmitted to us worthy of regard and veneration — condemning no established institution, opinion, or usage because it is old, provided it possess the elements of true value, and the genuine stamp of excellence — and tolerating none, whether new or old, which can not endure the searching ordeal of investigation, and abide the severest test of a sound and enlightened reason.

CHAPTER VII.

METHODS OF INTELLECTUAL CULTURE.

THE principal object of public school instruction, as has already been remarked, is intellectual culture. Moral and religious instruction, however important and indispensable in the formation of character, can only be incidentally communicated. The character of the teacher, the influences of the school-room—the requisitions of order, obedience, quiet and respectful deportment, truth, honesty, self-control, the faithful performance of all prescribed duties—and the religious exercises at the opening and closing of the school, are the chief agencies by which in these institutions the moral and religious faculties of the pupil can be strengthened and matured. The prominent and special work to be done is the cultivation and discipline of the mind—first, by the positive communication of the elementary principles of knowledge, and then by the development and expansion of the faculties of reason, judgment, and discrimination, by such methods as shall most certainly and effectually conduce to the investigation and attainment of truth in any and every department of inquiry.

The mathematical sciences—those which treat exclusively of the relations, combinations and results of number and magnitude—such as arithmetic, algebra and geometry, admit of the attainment of absolute certainty, by a series of operations, starting from self-evident axioms and propositions and terminating in positive and incontrovertible conclusions; and whatever reasoning or demonstrations are based upon these sciences, have the stamp of indubitable truth, and are universally admitted. No one thinks for a moment of questioning the theory or the fundamental laws of gravitation discovered by Newton through the agency and upon the basis of rigid mathematical demonstration. No one disputes the laws which Kepler has announced as governing the movements and regulating the distances of the planetary orbits. No one controverts any of the great discoveries of Copernicus, Galileo, Tycho Brahe, the Herschels, Rosse or Le Verrier—for the simple reason that all these discoveries were based upon the most rigid mathematical demonstration applied to facts thoroughly and accurately observed.

The same facts and observations are open to all, and the demonstrations may be verified by all. The results have, consequently, passed into the domain of ascertained and settled truths, and remain forever as the heritage of all succeeding generations. In like manner those scientific discoveries, which, although not founded upon strict mathematical demonstration, rest upon sound deductions from ample and accurate observation, and which may also be at any time verified by similar observation and experiment, such as those which form the staple of all the natural sciences, have been elevated into the clear region of absolute and unquestionable truth—admitting indeed of farther expansion and more extended application, as additional discoveries resting upon the same basis are from time to time made, but defying contradiction or scepticism as to the results actually obtained or the laws or principles involved in those results. The mechanical laws and resulting phenomena, the principles of optics and their application to vision, the laws of light and color—of electricity in its multifarious forms and combinations, of steam with all its grand results—of magnetism, electro-magnetism and magnetic electricity, with their far-reaching consequences in spanning the circumference of the globe by a chain of electric thought—of geology, with its ancient records extending through countless ages before the existence of humanity—these, together with the grand and marvelous results which the telescope and the microscope have opened up to us, are unquestioned, undenied and undeniable. They are portions of the aggregate stock of human knowledge, free and open to all, with the indelible stamp of truth and certainty permanently affixed to their promulgation and diffusion. However we may wonder at their disclosures—however we may be startled by new and astounding developments from these and similar ascertained principles and laws, neither the laws nor their results admit of question or dispute. Their verification is within the reach of all; and we unhesitatingly accept them as facts upon which we may certainly and uniformly rely.

There is, however, another class of questions which present themselves constantly in the experience of every one, demanding our solution and requiring our judgment and determination, in order that we may also, if possible, place the results in the category of ascertained knowledge. These questions do not admit of mathematical demonstration, nor can they in the great majority of instances be referred to settled scientific principles for their determination. The manner in which we dispose of them, and the conclusions to which we arrive, may and frequently do affect to a very important extent our conduct, our principles, our character, and the general current and results of our lives, and exert a powerful influence upon our happiness and well-being. Nay, more—they may and frequently do seriously affect the condition of communities, the progress of civilization, and the fortunes of the human race. They may relate to the passing events of every-day life, or to the more grave and serious problems of Christianity, philosophy, political and social economy, civil government, and civil and religious institutions of every grade. They may involve personal and private interests, or the great issues of peace or war, liberty or slavery, free trade or commercial restrictions, free institutions or governments wanting the essential elements of freedom. In short, they may have only an individual bearing, or they may affect us seriously in our relations to our fellow-men, to the community in which we live, to our country, to the world at large, and to our Creator. Now in order to solve these various questions, and to ascertain the results with as near an approximation to absolute truth as is possible in a class of cases where positive certainty is unattainable, it is conceived to be only necessary to apply the same *method* of procedure as in purely scientific investigations. To do this, however, we must train our minds by a rigid and severe process of inductive and deductive reasoning to the thorough analysis of the problem before us, whatever may be its nature; we must accurately observe and carefully note every fact and every principle having any, the remotest, bearing upon it, giving to each its due weight, and no more; we must eliminate, with stern and unflinching severity, every element of error, every prejudice, preconception, or misconception, which may have crept into our minds; and must approach the consideration of the various questions presented, as far as may be possible, with the same coolness, and the same indifference to the result, provided only the truth be ascertained, which characterize the proceedings of the inventor or discoverer in the fields of scientific research. All this may be exceedingly difficult, and well-nigh impossible, especially in the discussion of questions involving great principles or paramount interests, individual, moral or social; and yet it is the only mode in which certainty can be attained, and error avoided.

The proper discipline and training of the mind

in the process of intellectual education involves, therefore, the necessity of accustoming the pupil, first, to the habit of *accurate observation.* Whatever may be the subject-matter under consideration, whether the solution of a mathematical or geometrical problem, the analysis and application of any ordinary or extraordinary question of fact in the every-day affairs of life, the validity or invalidity of any alleged principle or doctrine in political or social economy, in statesmanship, legislation, literature, or art, *clear and accurate observation of the actual facts or phenomena* is indispensable to any valid progress or reliable conclusions. This habit may be formed at a very early period in the education of the child, and should pervade its entire course, from the earliest lessons of the primary school to the termination of the highest course of instruction. No fact, however apparently unimportant, coming under consideration or discussion, or presented by the text-book, should be permitted to be dismissed without thorough and careful analysis—without being, if possible, fully comprehended and understood *in its simple aspect as a fact,* independently of its particular bearings, or the particular use to be made of it. The simple questions at this stage of the investigation should be, What is it? What are the exact phenomena presented? *What are the facts?* These questions being satisfactorily answered, and duly noted, the induction from the facts is appropriate. But the two processes must be kept entirely independent of each other. The *particular fact* observed is one thing—the *conclusion* or *deduction* to be drawn from it, whether by itself alone or in conjunction with other observed facts—essentially another. The existence and value of the former has no dependence whatever upon the accuracy or inaccuracy, the soundness or the unsoundness, of the latter. Each must rest upon its own proper basis. Innumerable illustrations will readily occur to every reflecting mind, of the fallacies and errors resulting from a combination of these two processes. Certain appearances present themselves with which we have been accustomed to connect the idea of certain objects or certain consequences. We carefully observe and note all these appearances, and our analysis of all the observed phenomena may be strictly accurate. Yet we may err in pronouncing at once upon those appearances that the conclusion which immediately suggests itself is the true one. In order to do this, it may be necessary to subject the facts presented to a variety of searching tests, in order to determine, with *cer-*

tainty, their connection with the supposed results, and whether they may not really consist with other and different conclusions. The facts really observed remain unaffected by this additional process—the conclusions are the results of a new and additional analysis. Still more familiar illustrations may be formed in the numerous well-attested cases, in courts of justice, of fatally erroneous judgments, based on apparently the clearest circumstantial evidence. It will readily be perceived that the important distinction here referred to materially affects the value of all human testimony; and that in determining upon the credit to be given to any narration, the facts actually observed must be cautiously separated from the induction, or inferences drawn from and intermingled with those facts. From inattention to or neglect of this essential element of reasoning, innumerable errors have in all ages been perpetuated, fatal injustice done to innocent individuals, and the interests of truth and knowledge sacrificed to a hasty and an unjustifiable generalization from undoubted facts to illegitimate and wrong conclusions.

In the intellectual process of *induction*, as well as in that of observation, the mind, in order to arrive at exact truth, must be divested of all passion, prejudice or bias. It must come to the investigation of facts and the induction of consequences or results, with entire freedom to accept the facts as they shall actually be found to exist, and the inferences or conclusions as they shall develop themselves in accordance with the principles of sound reasoning. It must have no preferences for one description of facts more than for another. Truth is simple and indivisible; as unbending and severe in its relations to questions involving the highest interests and welfare of individuals and communities as to those which relate only to mathematical combinations or scientific principles. And hence it is, that while in the domains of scientific research, dealing with abstract numbers or lines, and the principles and laws of matter and of motion with their applications and results, knowledge has advanced with such rapid strides as to exceed the most sanguine anticipations of the most advanced intellect, while in other fields of investigation, where the feelings, the passions, the prejudices, or the interests of individuals are in any manner affected, the establishment and settlement of great principles of morals, legislation, society and government can only be accomplished after centuries of controversy, error and wrong. While the magnificent discoveries in astronomical science have enabled us to gaze upon the marvelous harmonies of infinite space, and to calculate the distances and analyze the movement and constituent elements of constellations, of suns so far removed from the utmost boundaries of our own system that light, with its immense velocity of nearly two hundred thousand miles a second, requires hundreds of years to span the interval—while the patient researches of the geologist has enabled us to trace the history of our own planet, through the ineffaceable records of the rocks, over a period extending through the lapse of incalculable ages—and the indomitable energy and perseverance of the devotees of mechanical science have brought the very elements into subserviency to the will and the wants of humanity—while all these grand and sublime results have been achieved by the intellect of the race, acting in strict accordance with the laws of thought, how is it with those great questions which underlie the happiness and prosperity of individuals, nations, and humanity at large, and which have been agitated and discussed from the earliest dawn of civilization, through all the intervening years of suffering, tumult and hope? In the earliest annals of the world, the appeal to brute force, the "trial by battle," the decision by the sword, served to settle all controversy; and still the fertile plains of Europe and America are drenched with blood, to accomplish the same end. Then the bonds of slavery were riveted on the hapless captives of the sword; and slavery has but recently been extinguished by a prolonged and desperate struggle, involving in its results hecatombs of human lives, and threatening the very existence of the government under which we live. The fundamental principles of government are yet undergoing discussion—the laws of trade, international law, civil and criminal law, far from being settled, are constantly subjected to important modifications; nor have any definite or satisfactory results been attained in reference to the grave question of education, and the relation which exists between the social and domestic institutions of every civilized community, and the intelligence and happiness of the individuals who are brought within their pale. Governments and political economists are still widely divided in opinion as to the expediency and wisdom of free trade or commercial restrictions, and if restrictions must exist, whether the interests of individuals and associations, or the financial arrangements of governments shall primarily or chiefly be consulted. Legislators and philanthropists have failed to determine whether the infliction of the penalty of death is imperatively demanded for the commission of even the highest crimes known to the law. The right of every child to such an education as shall enable him to comprehend and properly to discharge every duty incumbent upon him, as a future citizen and member of society, and the reciprocal obligation of communities and states to furnish such an education, are as yet practically acknowledged to a very limited extent only, either in Europe or America. Innumerable questions of minor importance, but affecting extensively the conduct, character and well-being of the race, are still agitated and discussed, with but a remote prospect of definitive determination. The relations between crime in its various grades, its prevention and punishment, and the reform and restitution to society of its perpetrators; the important problem of pauperism—of the means for its prevention and alleviation, wholly or in part; in short, all the various problems of society, government, legislation, ethics, political economy and morals, which during the past three centuries have occupied the minds of mankind, —each and all are legitimately within the province of the intellectual faculties, and each and all *admit* of a definite and clear solution, provided only the same *method* and processes of induction, deduction and reasoning which govern the reasonings, inferences and conclusions of scientific men in matters pertaining to the physical relations of the universe, are faithfully applied.

It is not because there is any intrinsic or insuperable difficulty in the collection, observation and analysis of facts or phenomena in the class of cases under consideration—nor because there is any invincible obstacle to their comparison and generalization or to the inferences and deductions to be drawn from them by a clear and sound process of reasoning—that they have not yet been brought within the domain of ascertained knowledge, and placed upon the broad foundation of truth and certainty. It is because, and only because a dense and powerful element of error, in the guise of interest, ignorance, prejudice, preconception or passion, in some or all of their numerous forms, has distorted and perverted the facts, clouded the reasoning and falsified the conclusion. The scales of observation and induction, which should have been so accurately constructed and so nicely poised as to represent the exact value of each fact, and the weight of each inference "even to the avoirdupois of a single hair," have consciously or unconsciously been heavily burdened with incongruous ingredients, and tampered with by malign influences; and the result is utterly untrustworthy. When Harvey announced to the world his great discovery of the circulation of the blood, an entire generation was destined to pass before the disappearance of these discordant elements permitted the full admission and undoubting reception of this important truth; and yet, during this whole period, the facts upon which it was based, and the legitimate and necessary inferences from those facts, were as open to the observation and reasoning of every cultivated mind as to that of the illustrious discoverer. It was always true and susceptible of the most rigid demonstration, that the planets revolved in a fixed and definite orbit around the sun as their common centre; and yet the prevalence of ignorance, error and prejudice prevented for more than three thousand years the universal recognition of that great central fact of astronomical science. In like manner all conceivable problems in morality, ethics, legislation, government, political or social economy, intellectual or moral philosophy, have and can possibly have but one true solution; and the materials for that solution are accessible to every enlightened and properly disciplined mind. Truth is one and indivisible—

the same yesterday, to-day and forever—and its mountain summits tower far above and beyond the region where the dark clouds of passion, prejudice and error intercept or distort the bright radiance of its beams.

The great end then to be kept in view in intellectual education should be, the systematic development of the faculty of *strict logical reasoning from accurately ascertained premises*—the careful elimination, either in the investigation of facts or the inductions or inferences drawn from them, of every element of prejudice, passion, or interest—and the attainment of the power to arrive by these means to the utmost possible approximation to absolute truth, of which the nature of the problem under consideration, whatever it may be, will admit. There may be and are questions in which perfect certainty is unattainable—questions, the complete solution of which transcends and must ever transcend our unassisted human faculties. These problems pertain to a higher region of being—a higher province of thought and action. The mental powers bestowed upon us here, however capacious they may be or may become in their highest development and culture, have yet their boundary, beyond which they are incapable of passing. Within those boundaries however they may be enabled, by severe discipline and thorough cultivation, to attain to positive knowledge, scientific, ethical or practical, where *all the facts* or phenomena on which their decision depends, are accessible.

Correctness and accuracy of observation, careful discrimination of difference, comparison, induction and generalization, may therefore and should form an indispensable part of all school instruction. Beginning in the primary departments with the most familiar and well-known objects — the furniture in the school-room, the forms, dimensions, structure, color, uses, and objects of the various articles submitted to inspection—passing on to pictorial representations of animals, minerals, and vegetables, trees, fruits, flowers, etc., with the originals of which the pupils are more or less acquainted, subjecting these to the same process of analysis, description and induction — and gradually extending the course to embrace every thing of interest and importance within the range of the awakened faculties of the young learner—it is easy to perceive that a most valuable foundation may in this way be laid by faithful and competent teachers for future efforts of observation, reason and judgment. Keeping these principles and methods of teaching steadily in view throughout the entire course of instruction, let every sentence that is read in the text-book be thoroughly comprehended and understood, every lesson completely mastered, and every process of reasoning, demonstration, induction or inference accurately followed, and no advancement permitted until every previous step has been firmly planted. Let the teacher see that every false and erroneous conception is carefully corrected—every fallacy detected and set aside—every conscious or unconscious element of prejudice, preconception, feeling or passion eliminated—and every energy and faculty wholly directed to the ascertainment of truth—and to the attainment of sound and accurate knowledge.

This process must at first, and perhaps for a long time, be slow: its successive steps will require great patience, perseverance, and care. Too much must not be undertaken at once, and too much must not be expected. The results will, however, amply repay the expenditure of time and labor bestowed. The faculties of the expanding intellect must on no account and on no pretenses be overtasked. Frequent opportunities for relaxation and recreation should be afforded, and an alternation of studies requiring different degrees of attention and different methods of illustration will be found to afford very sensible relief. The mind requires rest after continued tension for a longer or shorter period no less than the body; and change or variety of occupation not unfrequently produces as salutary an effect in both as entire repose or inaction. In the case of great activity of the mental faculties, such an alternation, judiciously arranged, exerts even a far more beneficial tendency than entire inaction or mere recreation. Every well-constituted mind requires constant exercise, in some direction, of its various faculties, and although the long-continued exertion of its energies upon any one subject of thought, reading or study produces weariness and fatigue, yet the experience of every student demonstrates that the temporary abandonment of that subject and the substitution of some other, demanding or permitting a new and different channel of mental effort, will restore the equilibrium, and supply the necessary relaxation of the faculties which have been tasked to their utmost capacity. In any case, pure mental idleness—utter vacuity or indolence of mind—should never be encouraged or tolerated. A systematic and judicious course of study should be marked out, so arranged as to occupy all the portion of the day not devoted to other pursuits, including physical exercise and relaxation, and so distributed as to afford, at intervals of not exceeding one hour, such an alternation of studies and literary pursuits as will effectually preclude mental fatigue, and secure a vigorous and wholesome tension. The early morning hours should be consecrated as far as practicable to the more abstruse and difficult studies—those which require a greater concentration of the mental energies—while the residue of the day may be profitably devoted to those departments of literature which make less demand upon the higher faculties of thought. All serious intellectual exertion should be laid aside for at least one hour before retiring to rest, to afford nature uninterrupted opportunity for that complete renewal of the exhausted mental and bodily functions which is equally indispensable to physical health and mental well-being.

Thus by the mutual co-operation of the parent, teacher and pupil, guided by a carefully-considered and well-matured system, and keeping constantly in view the whole complex nature of the being, all whose faculties—physical, intellectual, moral and social—are to be developed, disciplined and directed, the great work of EDUCATION may be satisfactorily accomplished, and the spring-time of life, while in no respect deprived of its exuberant sources of happiness and enjoyment, consecrated to its legitimate task of preparation for a bountiful and abundant harvest of usefulness, honor and fame.

CHAPTER VIII.

MORAL AND RELIGIOUS INSTRUCTION.

IT has been made a serious and important question in what manner and to what extent moral and religious instruction can be communicated in our public schools. On the one hand it has been contended that the chief if not the sole object of these institutions is purely secular instruction—that the inculcation of morality, except so far as it is involved in the ordinary and necessary discipline of the school, or comes up incidentally in the prescribed course of instruction, is not within the range of the duties committed to the teacher; that the fundamental truths of Christianity are so diversely held and interpreted by different individuals and religious sects, that it is exceedingly difficult, if not impossible, to illustrate and enforce them free from sectarian bias; and that, therefore, the whole domain of moral and religious instruction properly appertains to the family and to the Church, where the peculiar views and doctrines of each parent can be distinctively and fully taught.

On the other hand it is alleged that the very idea and the essential object of education consists in the development and cultivation of every faculty of the human mind; that to confine its office exclusively or chiefly to the mere communication of secular knowledge and the discipline of the intellectual powers, is unjustifiably and injuriously to restrict its appropriate province; that the early, continued and judicious culture of the moral and religious faculties of our nature is of vital importance, and indispensable to the foundation of a good character and the attainment of our happiness and well-being here and hereafter; that to leave out of view this essential element in any course of instruction designed to exert an important and controlling bearing upon the whole of future life, is inevitably to give a wrong and distorted direction to the mind, while it fatally injures the moral nature; that the teacher to whom is confided the education of the young stands in this respect in the place of the parent, in regard as well to moral and religious instruction as to intellectual culture, and while he has no right to interfere with the conscientious convictions or peculiar religious belief of such parent, or to instill into the minds of his pupils any denominational or sectarian views, it is his duty to inculcate those great fundamental principles of Christianity in which good men of every denomination concur, and which admit of no dispute or diversity of opinion; that without alluding to those controverted topics, which have in all ages divided the religious world, the teacher may find ample scope in the Christian Scriptures for the illustration and enforcement of all those truths which lie at the foundation of Christian morality, and that no education is worthy of the name which does not aim at the elevation and improvement of the moral and spiritual as well as the intellectual being, or does not cultivate, refine and purify the affections and the heart at the same time that it informs and strengthens the mind.

Fully concurring in these views, and profoundly sensible of the importance of moral culture, based on the sound foundation of Christian civilization, in all our systems of popular education and public instruction, I deem it incumbent on me to present some practical suggestions in reference to the order and method in which this culture may best and most effectually be communicated.

The first indispensable ingredient in this great work is the character and deportment of the teacher. The influence of example on the minds and hearts of the young is boundless and incalculable. The child who in the domestic circle is permitted to see and hear nothing but wretchedness and strife and anger and harsh revilings, insensibly imbibes evil principles, and becomes assimilated to the moral atmosphere by which it is constantly surrounded. On the other hand, the inmate of a happy home, where mutual affection, sympathy and love abound—where the eye, from earliest infancy, rests only upon spectacles of physical and moral beauty, and the ear is greeted only by the accents of benevolence and kindness, needs no other incitement to pleasurable and virtuous activity, and forms no other wish or desire than to deserve the approbation of those to whom it is indebted for so much of happiness and enjoyment. Both these classes and numerous intermediate ones, in every gradation of life and character, are, at an early age, transferred for several hours of each successive day to the teacher's care. If, therefore, the moral atmosphere of the school-room is what it should be—if the teacher possesses those attributes which intuitively and spontaneously command deference and respect—

if firmness and authority be tempered with mildness and uniform kindness, and the requisite capacity for communicating knowledge be combined with an invincible patience, rigid impartiality, undiscriminating attention and regard, and unwearied perseverance in overcoming the innumerable obstacles to intellectual progress which present themselves on every hand, the transition from home—whether that home be virtuous or vicious—becomes an onward and an upward step in the journey of life.

Order, obedience, and system should demand the teacher's earliest and most earnest attention. Each pupil, of whatever grade, age or condition, should be made to understand, on his first entrance into the school, that unhesitating, unquestioning obedience to its rules, regulations and discipline will be rigidly required, and undeviatingly enforced; that the exercises of the school must be conducted with perfect order and uniformity, and that an intelligible and enlightened system must, in all things, be adhered to. Nothing is so fatal to the success or so paralyzing to the usefulness of a school, as the absence or general relaxation of discipline. The will of the teacher must be paramount—his orders must at all hazards be obeyed—order must be preserved, or anarchy, confusion and discord must be the inevitable result. The tendency of the age in which we live is, it is greatly to be feared, to habits of insubordination, irreverence, and disrespect to all established authority, however sacred or venerable. The absorbing devotion to the pursuit of wealth, honors and station which has so strikingly characterized the past half-century, especially in our own land and under the influence of our free institutions, has sensibly loosened those wholesome and salutary restraints of domestic discipline which are so essential to the formation of habits of order and a proper regard for the rights and interests of others, and of the community to which we belong. A large and constantly increasing class of youth is springing up in our midst, and exerting a most deleterious influence upon the morals of our land, with whom nothing is sacred, nothing venerable, nothing worthy of deference or respect. Self-emancipated from all parental control, long before a solitary principle of virtue, or a single habit of order, industry or system could be inculcated, these precocious representatives of a prurient and new-fangled civilization, the rank growth of a poisonous infidelity and an inexcusable idolatry of wealth, plunge recklessly into all the excesses and dissipations of the metropolis—sound all its depths of infamy and licentiousness—spurn all control—trample upon every obligation of duty—and speedily find their way to the prison, the penitentiary, and the gallows. So general and potent is this influence, favored as it is by the criminal negligence and indifference of parents, that even where some degree of restraint is exercised, and the sanctuary of home is still retained, loose principles of action are imbibed, habits of indolence, sensuality and sloth induced, irreverence and disrespect inculcated, and all the graces, amenities and sanctities of life abjured and discarded. And these, and such as these, are the youth who, in a few brief years, are to succeed to the solemn responsibilities and duties of citizens—to give an impulse and a direction to the government under which we live—to aid in moulding the civilization of the age, and shaping the future destinies of the race! They throng the streets and crowd the avenues through which we daily pass to our counting-houses, our offices and shops—bold, impudent, noisy, riotous, blasphemous, and lost to all sense of decency or self-respect—they congregate in crowds wherever the opportunities and materials for low dissipation and vicious indulgences are to be found; and we know that from these baleful nurseries of vice and crime the murderer's deadly weapon, the incendiary's torch, the robber's stealthy devices, the pugilist's disgusting and shocking brutality, the drunkard's haggard debauchery, the libertine's unhallowed orgies, and all those elements of degradation and of evil which wither and blast human society and human intercourse, proceed and have their origin; and yet we pass them by, content to know that as yet our own homes are unviolated, our own persons safe, our treasures unattacked, our interests unassailed! Friends of education! teachers, parents, Christians, lovers of order, sobriety, and peace — shall this state of things be permitted to continue, and to diffuse its poisonous and contaminating influence over the entire surface of our modern civilization? or shall the youth of our land be gathered as one great family into our public schools, and there be taught habits of order, principles of obedience, and reverential respect to established authority, sentiments of virtue, nobility, and a manly ambition for excellence and all those Christian graces which elevate and adorn the character, and conduce to future greatness and happiness?

Earnestness of purpose should also be assiduously and practically incul̓cated upon the expanding minds of youth. The teacher should avail himself of every suitable occasion to impress upon his pupils the importance, necessity and utility of that single-minded consecration of all their energies to the task before them; that concentration of their faculties—that undivided attention—that *earnestness* of effort which alone can ensure success. Nothing is more common in schools of every grade than lassitude of mind and indolence of effort; that aimless, careless, desultory and fitful application to study which proclaims it, manifestly, an irksome and unwelcome task instead of a pleasure. This may, indeed, occasionally be the result of physical causes, demanding a prompt and efficacious physical remedy, but more frequently has its origin in mental indisposition arising from failure to appreciate the true nature and object of the exertion required. It should be the aim of the teacher to supply this stimulus, to inspire in the mind and will of the pupil the requisite ambition, and to concentrate his energies upon the acquisition of whatever purpose he desires to accomplish. Whoever is thoroughly in earnest in the pursuit of his object, whatever it may be, possesses in himself an impulse which has power to overcome mountains of opposition and to annihilate the most formidable obstacles.

Sincerity, conscientiousness, and a strict regard to truth, under all circumstances, should be cultivated and required. In the ordinary intercourse of the school-room innumerable occasions present themselves for ascertaining the characters and dispositions of the pupils in these respects, and for testing the strength of their incipient principles. These occasions should be promptly and skillfully seized; the wavering virtue of the tempted fortified and strengthened—adherence to the rigid rules of rectitude encouraged and sustained—duplicity, tergiversation and falsehood sternly but temperately rebuked and uniformly discountenanced, and the whole force of that "public opinion," which is as potent and efficacious in the school-room as in a more extended and advanced field of action and of effort, brought to bear upon the pertinacious offender. The conscience and the reason should be affectionately, firmly, and judiciously appealed to; the moral sensibility awakened and excited; the affections enlisted; and every accessible ally pressed into the service of truth and virtue against the strongest allurements of appetite, inclination and passion. Let the teacher never despair of reclaiming the most obstinate and vicious by persevering and practical appeals to the intellectual and moral nature. The result may not be speedily attained, and the process may require the most patient and trying continuance of effort, but some master-chord of the heart will be found sooner or later to respond to the Ithuriel spear of affectionate remonstrance, and a human and immortal soul be saved, it may be, from destruction and ruin.

One of the most common and injurious errors in the discipline of youth consists in the vain attempt to suppress the activity of those energies and passions, the ordinary manifestations of which are indicative of an evil and vicious tendency. The almost invariable effort of this injudicious training is to strengthen and confirm the inclination we desire to subdue, even though we succeed in repressing its outward action. Each passion and faculty of our nature has its appropriate field of exertion, and each instinctively demands its proper gratification. It is our duty as parents and teachers to recognize this fundamental principle of humanity, and while we discountenance and check every excessive or improper manifestation of any mental or moral power, we should divert its activity and direct its energies into safe and legitimate channels. The observation or neglect of this principle involves consequences in the future of most momentous import to the happiness and well-being of the child. The same powers, propensities and passions which, properly and judiciously directed and applied, constitute the ardent and effective reformer, the sagacious and discriminating statesman, the astute diplomatist, the energetic and enterprising man of business, the bold, fearless and indomitable patriot, may be converted through unrestrained indulgence or unwise repression and constraint into those fatal and destructive elements of vice and crime which signalize the unprincipled career of the reckless violator of his country's laws, and the abandoned victim of depravity and guilt. The exuberant impulses of an active, ardent, restless spirit, in the unthinking, uncalculating impetuosity of its youthful and inexperienced energies, are but too often mistaken for the deliberate promptings of lawless will and vicious inclination; and many a noble mind and generous heart, capable of the most exalted excellence, has been fatally and irreclaimably perverted and ruined for want of a discriminating appreciation of those true and genuine tendencies which only needed proper indulgence and direction to ripen into useful, honorable and noble exertion. Let it never be forgotten that the elements of goodness, virtue and excellence are implanted by the Creator in every human spirit; and that it is the special and peculiar function of the teacher to discover, to develop, and to cultivate and direct these precious germs, however deeply encrusted in ignorance, overlaid by passion, or surrounded by thick and tangled weeds of vice. Deep in the breast of the most incorrigible and depraved there are yet fountains of living waters, accessible, it may be, only to the profoundest observation and most skillful research, but of power to renovate, to cleanse, purify and invigorate the whole moral being.

Deference and regard to the wants and convenience of others, self-denial and uniform good temper in all their intercourse with their associates should be made to characterize the deportment of the pupils of every school-room. By insisting upon this as a rule admitting of no exceptions, teachers will essentially promote quietness and order, while at the same time they will be laying the foundations of an elevated, noble and disinterested character to those committed to their charge. Of all the traits which serve to harden the heart and debase the affections in after life, selfishness is at once the most common and most fatal. Developing itself as it does at the earliest dawn of consciousness, it is too frequently stimulated into excessive and inordinate action by the injudicious fondness and partiality of parents—and gaining strength with years, it soon comes to exercise a powerful and most deleterious influence upon the character and habits. The wants and claims of others are unfelt and disregarded; the channels of sympathy and mutual regard are effectually closed up; the engrossing demands of self-interest, personal convenience and individual gratification take precedence of every consideration of justice, generosity and kindness; and the worst passions of our nature are enlisted in support of these inordinate and extravagant pretensions. Society in all its departments—all our civil and social institutions, from the highest to the lowest, bear the impress of this all-prevailing evil. Christianity for eighteen centuries has protested against it in vain. The earliest lessons of childhood—the force of example—the incentives of passion—the love of dominion, and the pleasure of self-indulgence—have proved too powerful for the mild teachings of religion and philosophy; and one generation after another has transmitted its annals of wars, desolation, and conquest—of violence and blood—of strife, tumult, and confusion—all originating in selfishness, personal ambition, pride and passion, and perpetuated by that prevailing disregard for the interests and feelings of others, which seems in a measure forced upon us by the overwhelming pressure of the vast and complicated machinery of modern civilization. It is in our power, aided by the blessing of Heaven, essentially to mitigate, if we can not hope ultimately to remove, this calamitous evil, by early and constantly impressing upon the minds of each pupil committed to our charge the spirit of that divine precept of Christianity, "Whatsoever ye would that others should do to you, do ye even so to them"—by such a discipline of the intellect and of the heart as shall accustom each to prefer the interests and wants of others to his own—to overlook self in the earnest desire to be useful—to repress and subdue, in their earliest manifestations, the angry and vindictive passions—to cultivate and cherish habits of beneficence and benevolence—noble and generous impulses—lofty and disinterested traits of character—and to aspire to that excellence which, regardless of self, except so far as the welfare of others is concerned, places all its happiness and all its enjoyment in the ability to confer blessings upon all who come within the circle of its influence and its power. To this end, the example of the great and the good, which ancient and modern history afford, should be carefully cultivated, and frequently and earnestly dwelt upon. No opportunity should be lost on the part of the teacher of manifesting the importance and the beauty of this principle by such practical illustrations as the administration and discipline of the school-room and the passing events of the day may afford. That demeanor and deportment which the conventional rules of the best society require in the intercourse of refined life, and which is too often but the false and hollow substitute for the genuine feelings of the heart—too often worn as the mask and "counterfeit presentment" of virtue and goodness—should be rendered the natural and genuine manifestation of the character—the graceful and legitimate exponent of the dispositions and the affections.

I deem it unnecessary on the present occasion to go more into detail on these topics. In the various suggestions I have here thrown out, I am by no means unaware of the numerous and formidable difficulties which teachers will encounter in the endeavor to reduce them to practical effect. I am aware that they are required to deal with every variety of character and disposition; that innumerable obstacles are thrown in their path by the counteracting discipline of the family and the street; by the want of judgment, the want of time and attention of parents; by the force of long-cherished habits of indolence and vicious indulgences; and above all by the limited opportunities of systematic culture, which a due regard to other departments of duty leaves at their disposal. I am also fully aware that it is far easier to lay down general principles and rules than to carry them into practical effect. But it has occurred to me that even under all these embarrassments and obstructions the enlightened and faithful teacher may do much in educating and training the moral affections in those intervals of intellectual instruction which so frequently recur—that this instruction may itself be profitably interspersed with those precepts and practices which, judiciously and earnestly applied, may sink deep into the heart, and yield sooner or later an abundant and grateful harvest—and that in selecting the mode and the time for conveying these practical lessons of Christian morality, the judgment of each individual teacher may be put in requisition. I am mainly solicitous that whatever degree of mental improvement our youth receive in these elementary institutions of instruction should be based upon sound principles of moral culture — that the head and the heart, the intellect and the affections, the understanding and the will should be educated together in harmonious accordance with the demands of the entire nature. How this most desirable result may best be attained under the varying circumstances of each individual case, must be left in a great measure to the judgment and discretion of the teacher. Enviable, indeed, will be the feelings, and great the reward of that instructor, who, in looking back upon the long years of ill-requited toil and earnest effort in this noble profession, shall be able to trace to the lessons of the school-room the germs of future greatness, distinction and fame in the career of those minds destined to exert a lasting and a beneficial influence upon the human race—who, when some future Washington shall rise as the savior, deliverer, and lawgiver of his country — some future Hamilton, Jay or Clinton as its honored statesman—some Wilberforce or Howard as its philanthropist — some Milton, Shakespeare or Spenser as its poet—or some Bacon, Newton or Locke as its philosopher—shall be able with honest pride to point to yonder school, and to say, "It was there I first imbued his heart with the true conceptions of greatness—there the foundations of his towering intellect were laid upon the everlasting rock of Christian morality! There, under my teachings, the great ideas of human destiny and responsibility—the august vision of immortality—the noble ambition to live worthily and justly and usefully—to achieve eminence and distinction—to hand down to posterity an unsullied name and a cherished memory—first dawned upon his mental vision; and there, under my guidance, ripened, matured and expanded from day to day and year to year, until he went forth to the harvest-field of his greatness and his fame!" Earth has no nobler or higher triumph than this; and they who are thus instrumental in the humblest degree in leading "many to righteousness, shall shine like stars in the firmament for ever and ever!"

CHAPTER IX.

PRACTICAL EDUCATION.

IT is one of the most gratifying indications of the progress and advancement of the age in which we live that the public attention and regard is beginning to be more earnestly directed than it ever heretofore has been to the education of the people; that plans and systems of instruction, and principles of intellectual and moral culture are attracting more and more the public interest and attention; and that the press, the pulpit, and the other numerous organs of public sentiment that pervade our modern civilization, are beginning to discuss, with an animation and an energy reflecting the highest credit upon their motives, the best and most effectual mode of communicating knowledge to the youth of our land. These discussions necessarily partake of the spirit of the age, and are imbued to a greater or less extent with that peculiar coloring which emanates from the material tendencies of a rapidly progressive state.

Public sentiment demands, with increasing energy and emphasis in this our young republic, a *practical* education. In view of the circumstances by which we are surrounded—of the antecedents of our position—of the destiny we are required to fulfill—of the unprecedented progress of science, and the immense development and extension of art—it is insisted that public and private instruction should be conformed to the radical revolution which has thus been effected in the condition of the world—and should recognize the new tendencies of thought and action which have been developed by the events of the past hundred years. To this extent the demand is a reasonable one, and should undoubtedly be acceded to. But it does not stop here. In its excessive zeal for the reformation of those antiquated systems of instruction which were the growth and product of a less enlightened age, and which a more general diffusion of knowledge has rendered in some respects not only useless but pernicious, it applies the axe to the root of the tree, and demands the complete extirpation of that culture which the wisdom of our ancestors, for hundreds of generations, has regarded as indispensable to the formation of an elevating and commanding character. It finds no elements of beauty or of usefulness in those intellectual pursuits which have no immediate practical application to the every-day wants and requirements of active life. It discovers a vast and unbounded field of enterprise and exertion, opened up by modern science, the exploration and cultivation of which not only require but promise to repay the entire devotion of the mental and physical powers; and in all this ample field it finds no room for the abstruse researches of metaphysical philosophy, the erratic vagaries of the imagination and the fancy, the legendary lore of romance, the unrestrained flight of genius, the poet's rhapsodies, the musician's triumphs or the painter's skill. It has neither time to lose, energy to bestow upon, or faculties to appreciate the beauties or the sublimities of those old masters at whose consecrated shrine the literary world has worshiped for hundreds of centuries; nor does it desire to waste those precious hours in ideal reveries and impracticable day-dreams of beauty and perfection which may far more profitably be devoted to the acquisition and the retention of solid, tangible, material wealth, influence, power and station. It sees all around it the splendid results of worldly energy and enterprise, the brilliant triumphs of ambition, the stately palaces of wealth, the gorgeous trappings of power, and it recognizes in these the legitimate effects of that concentrated devotion to the useful, the attainable, the *practical*, which alone can ensure success in the crowded arena of modern civilization.

From this view of practical education I entirely dissent. I regard it as fatal to all true culture of the mind and the heart—destructive of all excellence—subversive of all nobility of character — and conducive, inevitably and irresistibly, to the gradual but certain decay of every generous impulse, every lofty aspiration of our nature. The faculties of our wondrous being are manifold and various, and in order to the harmonious play of the whole great fabric, each must be afforded scope for the full display of its powers. This world of flesh and sense which we inhabit, with all its pursuits, its toils, its aspirations and struggles and triumphs, can furnish adequate employment to a portion only of our capacities; and it is not all, even of life, to live. The attainment of wealth, the diffusion of knowledge, the progress of science and the arts, fame, station, influence, rank and power, are all but means to an ulterior and a noble end—the cultivation and proper employment of our rational and immortal nature. Whatever studies, occupations or pursuits most effectually advance this great end are most judicious and desirable, whether directly and immediately tending to our prosperity and success in the crowded avenues of every-day life or not. The lessons of Christianity, of philosophy and of experience have fallen upon strangely inattentive ears, if they have not taught us that the high places of the world, its glittering prizes and its loftiest honors, are not uniformly, or even generally, the reward so much of goodness, virtue, truth, integrity and wisdom, as of qualities with which these have but little connection or affinity. If to *succeed* in life be all our aim, if riches and honors and rank and station and power and influence constitute the El Dorado of our desires—the summit of our ambition, these objects may be and have not unfrequently been attained by the humblest intellect, with a very slight expenditure of mental cultivation or discipline.

There is, however, a view of practical education which is obnoxious to none of these objections. If it be meant that the youth of our land should be instructed in all those branches of science and of art which are indispensable to their future success in life—that they should be invested with the full and complete command of all their faculties—that they should be enabled promptly and skillfully to avail themselves, in any emergency, of those energies and powers of thought and of action which the crisis, whatever it may be, requires—that they should be familiarly acquainted with the results of past experience, and the amount of present knowledge in all those departments of scientific inquiry which the varied pursuits of life demand—and that they should be taught the relative importance and value of the different kinds of information and knowledge thus communicated—if this be what is meant by practical education, its value can scarcely be overestimated. If it be designed only to strike at the root of those ancient and exploded systems of learning which would sacrifice substantial attainments to empty show, and waste the precious years of youth in the laborious and irksome pursuit of useless and unavailable lore, and to reclaim for the careful and thorough investigation of the principles and problems of moral science a large proportion of that valuable time which has heretofore been monopolized by the classics, and by abstruse mathematical and metaphysical learning, a reform in this direction should be greeted and encouraged by the approbation of all reflecting minds. Those conservative influences which still cling with unyielding tenacity to routines of instruction which have long since lost their application to the requirements of the age, are pernicious in the extreme. They serve only to retard the progress of knowledge, and to cast insuperable obstacles in the path of literary and scientific advancement. In their inconsiderate zeal for the usages and customs of the past, their advocates and adherents are in imminent danger of losing sight of the present and the future; and in their strenuous efforts to arrest and fix the rapidly-revolving wheels of modern progress, they overlook the perilous hazards of so impracticable an enterprise. Nor is it to be regarded as at all wonderful that while the constituted guardians of Oxford and Cambridge, and other venerable and time-hallowed institutions of learning on both sides of the Atlantic, pertinaciously insist upon the virtual exclusion of all science not stamped with the credentials of the Middle Ages, the reaction of a more liberal and tolerant principle should verge to the opposite extreme. Accordingly the real danger, with which we in the present utilitarian age are threatened, is the too great and all-absorbing devotion of our energies to the practical pursuits of life; the entire subjugation of the ideal—not to the *real*, for this involves an admission we are not prepared to make—but to the *material*. In our judgment, education should embrace within its cognizance *all* the varied interests and pursuits of humanity, assigning to each its just proportion and influence, whether it has reference to the spiritual and immortal nature, or to the evanescent and perishable though not less real or pressing demands of time and sense. The imagination and the fancy, lawless and uncontrollable as may be their occasional flights, may yet be regarded as indispensable elements of our mental and moral being—bridging over, if we may be allowed the expression, the unfathomable abyss which separates the worlds of matter and of mind—the material and the spiritual—the seen and the unseen.

These high faculties of our nature must therefore be adequately provided for in every sound and well-considered system of education. To repress their manifestation—to deprive them of all opportunity of exertion—to clip their beautiful wings and debar them from that boundless empyrean of thought which constitutes their appropriate element—is essentially injudicious and injurious. The ideal, equally with the real, has its sphere of action and of enjoyment—a world of its own—scarcely less real, certainly not less important in its uses, than the material. Who shall undertake to limit the influence of those grand old masters of poetry and of song whose immortal strains have come down to us on the stream of time from the earliest ages of antiquity—meeting from age to age, in their magnificent course, responsive echoes in millions of human hearts, and sweeping onward in majestic grandeur to achieve in ages yet to come still nobler and ampler triumphs? Who shall tell how many minds have been exalted, purified and ennobled by those eloquent outpourings of genius and imagination which the rich stores of modern literature have supplied, and which, powerless as they may be in the thronged highways and byways of the world, exert a pervading and commanding influence over the hearts and lives of men? Beauty, too, is reflected in the handiwork of the Almighty Architect—from the lily of the valley to the illimitable expanse of the overhanging universe—scattered in boundless profusion wherever the eye can penetrate, or the imagination roam, and reproduced in fadeless tints on the immortal canvas of the great painters; sublimity, hushing every sense in breathless admiration, as the tremendous cataract dashes and plunges its mighty waters over the frowning abyss, and filling the mind with solemn awe as the fitful thunder-gust sweeps over the horizon. Who shall say these are not elements of powerful import in the constitution and culture of the human mind? And are these to be overlooked and neglected because they enter not into that account current of profit and loss which adjusts the dealings and regulates the intercourse of the practical world? Are all the nobler impulses of our being—the native instincts of immortality—the intuitive wanderings of the soul in quest of its mysterious destination—its heart-felt recognition of kindred and congenial elements in the good, the beautiful and the true—its sympathy with the familiar face of nature in its grandeur and its gloom, its majesty and sublimity, its universal and harmonious response when "touched to finer issues" by the master-hand of genius and of art—its thrilling susceptibility to kindness, to affection and love—its deep under-tone of sadness and lamentation, as the numerous ills of humanity pass in mournful review before it—and its restless aspirations after an excellence and a perfection unattainable here—are all these indications of a nature infinitely higher, nobler, purer than the "beggarly elements of flesh and sense," to be subordinated in our processes of education to the insatiable demands of a material age, or crushed beneath the remorseless wheels of that Juggernaut of wealth and power which the nations in these latter days have set up as the god of their idolatry?

No! a thousand times no! There is something within us which points to a loftier destination — a higher ambition than falls within the range of the boasted practical philosophy of the age in which we live. Our educational systems must indeed be reformed and renovated and reconstructed; but they must be elevated and not depressed. They must embrace the whole nature of man, develop all his faculties, bring into active exertion all his energies, and harmoniously adjust the balance of his higher and lower impulses. They must instruct him in the true value of his existence as an immortal being, and not the creature of a day or of an age. They must teach him that his mission here is one of self-discipline, of individual and mutual improvement, of usefulness to his kind, of comprehensive benevolence to his race, and not of selfish regard to his own distinctive interests, of systematic warfare against his fellows, of relentless oppression and cruelty and wrong. The eternal and immutable principles of justice, integrity, conscientiousness, reverence and regard for the rights of others must be inculcated; the passions trained to uniform subserviency to the reason and the judgment; the affections disciplined to the comprehensive law of love; the intellect enlightened to the clear perception and just appreciation of useful knowledge, and the will directed to the removal of every obstacle to the complete subjugation of evil in all its manifestations. Then, when the proud oppressor shall be forced to loose his grasp, and the chains of his helpless victim shall no longer be heard to clank—when violence and cruelty and injustice and wrong shall have withdrawn from our crowded marts and sought their native darkness and obscurity—when fraud and duplicity and falsehood and deception shall no longer stalk about with impunity and applause, and vice and infamy no longer rear their unblushing fronts in our temples of fashion and amusement—when the patriot and the statesman, the devoted philanthropist and the fearless reformer shall no longer be vilified, persecuted and contemned, and the high places of the land be no longer contaminated and defiled by corruption and wickedness and vice—when temperance and order and peace and concord and mutual esteem and brotherly kindness shall characterize the civilization of the age—then will Education have worthily fulfilled its high mission; then, indeed, will it have become *practical.* Till then the true teacher must labor on in faith and hope, patiently abiding his time and awaiting the harvest; unweariedly and diligently sowing the seeds of knowledge, of goodness and of truth, well-assured that all will not fall in stony places, and that a portion at least shall in due time "spring up and bring forth fruit—some thirty, some sixty, and some an hundred fold."

CHAPTER X.

FEMALE EDUCATION.

THE position which woman occupies in our modern civilization, and the influence she exerts, not only on the spirit of the age in which we live but especially and peculiarly on the character and conduct of the rising generation, demand on her behalf the most careful and comprehensive mental and moral culture which our systems of education can afford. The time has long since gone by—never to return—when her faculties were deemed incompetent to participate in that high intellectual discipline which we, the self-constituted lords of creation, saw fit to monopolize as our own peculiar and inalienable heritage. The Somervilles and Herschels and Mitchells, Baillies, Edgeworths and De Staels, the Hemans, Nortons, Sigourneys, Kirklands, Childs, Mitfords, and numerous other stars of the first magnitude in the scientific and literary horizon of the Eastern and Western Hemispheres, have secured for themselves and the sex they represent equal rank in the great constellation of genius and talent which adorns and illumines the age. Institutions of the highest grade for female instruction and education have arisen and multiplied themselves in Europe and America, until every vestige of that odious and unjustifiable distinction to which we have adverted in reference to the mental capacity of the sexes has disappeared. Indeed, the scales seem inclining of late to the opposite extreme, and pretensions to intellectual and moral *superiority* on the part of woman are gravely put forward and pertinaciously maintained. In these latter days of progress and advancement we are asked to make way in our legislative assemblies and councils of state for new and more competent as well as fairer elements of political economy, to open our busy marts of trade and commerce to the influx of these daring adventurers, and even to submit our own claims to a share in the administration of our civil and social as well as domestic institutions to the arbitrament by ballot of these insidious and enterprising rivals. In short—so formidable are the indications of the progress of this new power—we of the reigning dynasty, in whose hands the sceptre of government has from time immemorial been vested, have no other apparent alternative than at once and unconditionally to recognize the *claims* and admit the *rights* of our fair assailants to an equal participation of power, stipulating solely on our own behalf that it shall only be *exercised* with a due and becoming regard to the amenities and proprieties, the usages and customs of the domestic and social circle. We would not that our mothers, our sisters and our wives should so far diverge from the congenial and attractive quiet of their happy homes as to mingle in the din and turbulence of the hustings or the political assembly-room; nor have we as yet seen any evidence of their desire or inclination to do so. We deny the allegations to the contrary of those who claim to be their representatives in this behalf, and ask for their credentials. Is there one among the thousands of ladies engaged in our midst in the task of elementary instruction who craves the privilege of attending the polls on the days of our periodical elections, or who is anxious to address her fellow-citizens from the stump on the predominant issues of the day? Is there one among the tens and hundreds of thousands who preside over, adorn and elevate our happy homes and participate in their blessings, who would, if she could, enact the demagogue or conspicuously figure in our public journals as the public orator or declaimer, the successful or the unsuccessful candidate for the lowest or the highest station in the gift of his or *her* majesty, the people? Is there one who would willingly come down from the commanding elevation of womanly dignity, influence and unquestioned supremacy over the affections and the heart, that she might with impunity ascend the tribune or be invested with the insignia of legislative, judicial or executive powers? Or where is the true-souled, true-hearted woman who desires to be invested with the daily and harassing cares, vexations and responsibilities of commerce and trade, or to exercise the functions appertaining to any of the various professions? These are not the appropriate provinces of the sex, and no amount of conventional or other "agitation," no declamatory harangues in behalf of "woman's rights," or elaborate recapitulations of "woman's wrongs" can render them other than repugnant and distasteful. The true theatre of female influence and exertion is the domestic and social circle. These she is qualified to adorn, elevate and improve; and when she steps beyond these, she inevitably loses that attractive charm which places her beyond the reach of rivalry or competition in her own graceful and peculiar sphere.

While, therefore, we would not exclude woman from any field of intellectual or moral labor she may desire to occupy—while we would fully and unreservedly concede to her an entire equality of right with ourselves in all those departments of literary, scientific and artistical labor which conduce to the improvement and welfare of our common humanity—and while we would throw open to her free competition all those avenues of trade and business which may be occupied by her consistently with a proper self-respect and a due regard to the higher and nobler interests specially confided to her guardianship and care—we can not sympathize with that masculine enthusiasm, now so prevalent in certain quarters, which would give us, instead of the elevating and kindly influences of the domestic and social circle, an Amazonian phalanx, instead of homes lighted up, warmed and cheered by loving and beloved faces —a theatre of political intrigue and turbulent commotion,—instead of a sacred, inviolable, cherished asylum from the corroding cares, anxieties and oppressive burdens of the world, a counting-room, an office or a shop. We can not but feel that such a movement, under whatsoever specious pretense it may be impelled, in whatever philanthropic guise it may be clothed, would be a retrograde step in the world's civilization. We are not prepared for so radical and complete a revolution in all our preconceived ideas of the fitness of things. Nor do we entertain the slightest apprehension of its advent. A nobler and a grander destiny has been reserved for the women of the nineteenth century, and it is for that destiny we would have them educated.

There is no branch of human knowledge, no department of scientific instruction, no field even of professional labor or commercial or mechanical pursuits which should be excluded from the pale of female *education.* We would have our daughters, our sisters and our wives familiar, so far as may be practicable, with the fundamental principles of all the sciences and the practical operation of all the arts which conduce to human progress and advancement. We would have them intimately conversant with the great masters of poetry, philosophy and literary excellence of ancient and modern times; able to comprehend, appreciate and explain the profoundest speculations of the astronomer, the geologist, the chemist, the political economist, the metaphysician and the philosopher, and to extend, if need be, and push forward the researches of each into new and hitherto unexplored regions of matter or of mind, well versed in the history of the past, and competent to bring its instructive light to bear upon the incidents of the present and the prospects of the future, and familiarly acquainted with the constitutions, laws, institutions and governments of the various communities and countries of the world, and especially of our own.

Let it not be said that a course of instruction, full and complete like this, will unfit them for the discharge of the practical, every-day duties of life. All experience and history proves the contrary. Was Lady Jane Grey less qualified for usefulness in that station of life for which she was born—was she less amiable, less devoted to her husband and her friends, less capable of great actions and noble self-sacrifice to her convictions of duty, because she read Plato in the original Greek, and preferred conversing in solitude with that mighty mind to the frivolous amusements of her companions? Was Madame Roland less a heroine, less adapted to the difficult circumstances which surrounded her, less competent to administer consolation to her noble but ill-fated husband, and to sustain and support his drooping energies amid the calamitous scenes of that terrible Revolution, because of her splendid abilities and transcendent literary and scientific talents? Did Felicia Hemans struggle less heroically, devotedly and triumphantly against desertion, poverty and illness, or discharge less faithfully her duty to her helpless children because her cultivated intellect enabled her to soar upon the unflagging wings of the imagination into the loftiest and purest regions of poetical beauty and sublimity? Who will accuse Joanna Baillie, Maria Edgeworth, Amelia Opie, Mary Russell Mitford, Mary Somerville, Caroline Herschell, Mary Howitt, or our own Hannah Adams, Lydia Huntley Sigourney, Lydia Maria Childs, Caroline Matilda Kirkland, Miss Sedgewick, Harriet Beecher Stowe, and that radiant cluster of poetesses who beautify and adorn our intellectual galaxy, of inattention to the duties and claims of ordinary life? And if we are occasionally called upon to lament the perverse and erratic wanderings of a Martineau, a Trollope or a Fanny Wright, or to sympathize with the errors, the obliquities, the faults and the misfortunes of the Wolstoncrofts, the Godwins, the Nortons, and others like them, we console ourselves by the reflection that an unfavorable combination of circumstances, rather than any promptings of the intellect or the heart, darkened and obscured the path of these gifted daughters of genius, and intercepted those rays of happiness and enjoyment they were so well adapted to attract and to reflect. The want of congenial companionship, of a just and generous appreciation, of that kindness and affectionate regard without which the heart refuses to put forth its beautiful blossoms of hope and love — and above all the presence and pervading influence of sordid, base and groveling minds, of degrading and repulsive associations, and innumerable obstacles to the healthful development of the character and the intellect—all these sources of bitterness and disappointment are charitably and indulgently to be regarded.

It is undoubtedly true, however, that the graces of the intellect flourish and bloom in their perfection only when ripening and expanding in the clear and bracing atmosphere of moral virtue and Christian purity. We admire the brilliant and accomplished Aspasias, Zenobias, Cleopatras, Elizabeths, Catharines, Madame De Staels, but the heart goes forth to meet the mother of the Gracchi, the self-sacrificing Lucretia, the fearless and devoted Jeanie Deans, the fearless wife of La Roche Jaqueleine, the noble and heroic Grace Darling, and those pure-souled ministers of love and mercy, Florence Nightingale and our own incomparable Dorothea Dix. And who is there who does not revere the memory of Mary, the mother of Washington? or drop a tear of affectionate regard and veneration over the graves of those high-souled matrons who, in the darkest hour of our country's early history, supported the drooping energies of its champions, and cheered them onward to victory and to fame?

Our tenderest sympathies and deepest gratitude and affection accompany the members of that sisterhood of charity and Christian beneficence and love, which disarms sickness, disease and even death of half its bitterness and all its terrors; and yet in how many humble cottages, far removed from the noise and bustle of the world, and overlooked and forgotten by the busy multitude, dwell noble and self-sacrificing hearts, intent upon their mission of love, patiently and uncomplainingly watching over languid sufferers, silently enduring that "sickness of the heart" which comes from "hope deferred," and prospects blasted, and affections withered and wasted, and bravely and firmly bearing up against a fearful pressure of calamity, misfortune and wretchedness, admitting of no alleviation or consolation in the power of earth to bestow!

Nor is this ministry of these earthly angels confined to the cottages of the humble and the poor. In the abodes of wealth and luxury, in the stately mansion and the lofty palace, where riches and magnificence and grandeur and station and power abound, there comes a time when neither the towering intellect, nor the strong arm, nor all the treasures of the Indies, nor the trappings of rank, nor all the influence of greatness or of fame can avert the dread destroyer or postpone the inevitable hour. Then and there the quick eye of affection only can interpret the unutterable desire of the parting spirit; the hand of love only, calm the throbbing head and smooth the dying-pillow; the accents of the cherished, familiar voices of home alone, whisper peace and hope—that peace which "passeth all understanding"—that hope which "takes fast hold of immortality."

> "Oh, woman, in our hour of ease,
> Uncertain, coy, and hard to please,
> And variable as the shade
> By the light-quivering aspen made,
> When pain and anguish wring the brow,
> A ministering angel thou!"

This is the education which we would have every woman of our land to receive. An education which, while it shall develop and cultivate to their utmost capacity her intellectual powers and enable her to range at will over the ample and diversified fields of literature and science in all their varied manifestations, shall so train, discipline and direct her affections and her moral nature as to render her in the truest, noblest and highest sense a "helpmeet for man"—the effective participator, in her own appropriate sphere, of his toils and labors—the gentle and affectionate soother of his cares — the enlightened and congenial companion of his studies — the grace and ornament of his happy and cheerful home—the intelligent instructor and guide of his children—the devoted wife, mother and friend—the accomplished member of society, diffusing around her, wherever she moves, the fragrance, the beauty and the loveliness of virtue and Christian benevolence and beneficence. To her we would confide the education of our children, in the full and assured confidence that this sacred trust will be faithfully and conscientiously fulfilled. To her would we commit the guardianship of our homes, and as we unreservedly mingle in the crowded marts of business and the thronged highways of professional life, look forward with pleasant anticipation to the hour when we can divest ourselves of the irksome restraints and ever-recurring cares of the day, and repose our wearied spirits in the congenial and grateful atmosphere of domestic love and unchanging affection. With her would we renovate, purify and inform our minds and strengthen our hearts from those exhaustless fountains of wisdom and knowledge, fancy and imagination, beauty and sublimity, which ancient and modern literature supply, and with her drink deep from those perennial springs which "flow from Siloa's streams, fast by the oracles of God." Thus in life and in death—in prosperity and in adversity—in our hours of ease and enjoyment and happiness and tranquillity, and in the intervals of darkness and gloom and pain and suffering—mutually supporting and supported, giving and receiving the elements of joy and gladness, of consolation and sympathy—would we travel onward, side by side, hand in hand, fulfilling our mutual destiny in the communication of knowledge, the diffusion of virtue and happiness, the extension of science, and the elevation and improvement of our common humanity.

This is our theory of "woman's rights"—our ideal of female education. If a broader and more comprehensive "platform" can be constructed by the agitators and reformers of the day—of either sex—we are ready to accept it and to plant ourselves upon it whenever we shall become convinced that those for whom it is designed, and who are most interested in its construction, shall desire to avail themselves of its promised benefits. Till then we shall firmly adhere to those old and tried landmarks which the collective wisdom and experience of all preceding ages have consecrated — which sound philosophy approves, and the practical good sense of mankind confirms. When the day arrives — if it ever shall arrive — when woman "shoots madly from her sphere," and, abandoning that power and influence universally conceded to her over the hearts, the affections and the dispositions of man, asserts for herself an equality in those practical pursuits and employments for which he by nature and by education is peculiarly fitted—when she abandons the homes and hearths which she alone can render attractive, for the noisy turmoil and exciting scenes of restless ambition and the eager pursuits of business — when all that is beautiful and lovely and graceful in her character shall be exchanged for the base rivalries of opposing and conflicting interests, and the empty pride and vain pageantry of titles, distinction and wealth—then, and not till then, shall we be prepared to confess, with profound humiliation and contrition, that we had deplorably mistaken her inclinations, her affinities and her tendencies. Then, and not till then, shall we awaken to the melancholy consciousness of the deep delusion in which we have heretofore lived—to the baseless fabric of that golden dream of happiness and advancing knowledge and wisdom and power in which we had so long and so hopefully indulged.

CHAPTER XI.

THE TEACHER—HIS CHARACTER AND DUTY—MENTAL AND MORAL DEVELOPMENT.

THE process of education, as we have already seen, commences with the earliest inhalation of the vital element, and progresses with a constantly accelerated velocity, first under the auspices of the family circle, then of the elementary school and the family combined, and subsequently becomes matured in the great school of the world, or of that portion of it which bounds the experience of each individual, and comprehends the circle in which it is his destiny to move. Nor will this process be in any respect retarded by inattention, neglect or mismanagement, however much it may be guided, elevated, enlarged and directed by a wise vigilance and a discriminative culture. The work of education, either for good or for evil, so far as the individual who is the subject of it is himself concerned, will go on from birth to maturity, whether those whose appropriate duty and function it is to conduct its successive developments and shape its course faithfully discharge, or habitually neglect, or ignorantly or intentionally pervert the responsible trust committed to their charge. More than this. So sacred is the gift of an intelligent existence—so pure, holy and invigorating are all the ministrations of Nature and Providence—so uniformly and invariably is "the wind tempered to the shorn lamb"—that given the elastic energies of a sound and healthy physical constitution, and the ordinary intellectual and moral faculties, the positive exertion of some counteracting external agency is required to pervert, to weaken or extinguish the natural tendency to knowledge, to wisdom and virtue and happiness. The desire for knowledge is implanted in the human mind as one of its uniform and constituent elements, and the budding plant does not more naturally or invariably put forth its earliest energies in search of light, and its appropriate aliment, than does the expanding intellect grasp after knowledge—knowledge of itself—knowledge of the external world and all the manifold phenomena by which it sees itself surrounded. Full, however, as the world is of error, of vice and depravation and guilt, those counteracting tendencies which repress the growth of the mind, pervert its energies and lead it fearfully astray, seldom fail early to present themselves, even under the most favorable auspices, and to tinge with their dark hues the whole of future life.

In estimating the power and the effects of the best and the most skillfully devised system of education, we are apt to lay far too little stress on the circumstances by which we are constantly surrounded, and which, like the air we breathe and the infinitesimal particles of matter which incessantly float around us, are incorporated to a greater or less extent, at every moment of our existence, into our being. During that important portion of our lives ordinarily set apart for the specific communication of knowledge and moral and intellectual culture, these circumstances and associations are most powerful, impressive and efficacious in the formation and development of character, most tenacious in their hold upon our memory and our affections, and least capable of separation from the lessons with which they are accompanied.

Under these circumstances, neither the parent nor the educator can be said to have acquitted himself of the high responsibility which devolves upon him by the most systematic and clear communication of knowledge in any of its departments, or by the faithful and lucid exposition of moral truth, unless he has assiduously, patiently and perseveringly explored the depths of the mind he has undertaken to discipline and instruct—observed its constitution and its peculiar conformation—ascertained its elements both of weakness and strength—traced the principal dangers to which it is exposed from within and without—removed, so far as in him lies, the obstacles which impede its favorable development, or if that be found impracticable, furnished him with the mental and moral power either triumphantly to surmount or wisely to avail himself of those obstacles. The cultivator of the soil who should content himself with committing to the ground the best and most vigorous seeds, leaving them to germinate, expand and bring forth fruit, flowers and vegetables, without regard to any of the various circumstances which ordinarily impede or promote their growth, and claim, in virtue of this process, the meed of applause for his enlightened system of horticulture, would be guilty of no more fatal error and deserve no more signal disapprobation than would the educator or the parent, who, shutting his eyes to the ever-varying phenomena of surrounding circumstances, and the necessity of assiduous culture and constant supervision, expects from the most perfect system of intellectual instruction or moral ethics those just perceptions of truth and knowledge, and those harmonious proportions of character which constitute wisdom and virtue.

It is neither to be denied nor overlooked that "a change has come o'er the spirit" of that "dream" which, within the personal recollection of most of us, limited the mission and the functions of the teacher to the abstract communication of the mere elements of knowledge; to the preservation of a due degree of compulsory order within the repulsive precincts of the school-room, and to the fulfillment of the specific number of hours, days, weeks and months "nominated in the bond," by his personal attendance upon and supervision of a prescribed routine of tedious and monotonous exercises. It is not too much to say that an entire revolution in this respect has been effected within the last few years, and under our own immediate observation. In proportion as the value and importance of education has come to be recognized and understood in its relation to all our interests—personal and political, social, economical and religious—has the necessity been felt of availing ourselves of the highest moral and intellectual qualifications for the proper development and cultivation of the mental faculties of the rising generation. In proportion as the pages of history and our own observation and experience have forced upon us a clearer and deeper conviction of the great truth, that knowledge and virtue conjoined are absolutely indispensable to the happiness and prosperity, as well of communities and states as of individuals, has there been a deeper and more extended interest in the practical results of the elementary school, and in the degree of efficiency which it is capable of realizing.

No profession, no calling, can compare in utility, in the influence which it exerts, in the good which it can accomplish, in the evil which it can avert, in the prospects it can open up, in the happiness and well-being which it can secure, with that of the teacher. No profession, no calling, should be so honorable or so desirable—as none demands for its faithful and efficient fulfillment so much and such varied mental culture and discipline, so much moral worth, such unblemished purity of character and deportment, and such a combination of all the Christian virtues and graces. The reflex influence of these virtues and graces upon the affections, the heart and the life of the teacher is his highest and noblest reward.

Moral character is justly regarded as the first and most indispensable ingredient in the qualifications of a teacher. Without this the possession of the most finished learning, the most transcendent talents and the most perfect skill in communicating instruction would be valueless, and should be overlooked and disregarded. Those who are charged with the supervision of our elementary institutions of learning can not too strictly guard their portals from the contaminating influences of vice and immorality. Whatever other avenues the genius and spirit of our government and the free toleration of the age may have left open to those who have shaken off the obligations of virtue and honor and conscience, and who, by precept and example, contemn the salutary restraints of morality and Christian civilization, the haunts of youthful instruction should at least firmly and sedulously be closed against them. Whatever impurities the broad channel of human life in its swift and accumulating current may be destined to receive, as it rolls onward to the great ocean of eternity, let not its stream be poisoned at its sources. In the constantly recurring shocks and conflicts of the world, enough and more than enough of contamination will cling to the skirts of the most conscientious and pure-minded, without tainting the faculties of the mind and heart in their earliest development and expansion with a corruption which, it may be, not all the energies of an enlightened reason or an awakened conscience, not all the efforts of the most determined will can effectually obliterate or conceal.

In the midst of a community where the rank weeds of vice and crime abound in luxuriant and frightful profusion — where, however apparently fertile the soil, the seeds of goodness and justice and virtue are speedily choked and overborne by the poisonous tares of selfishness, of passion and of error in all its Protean forms — nothing less than a deep and abiding principle of religion and morality can enable us to realize the rich fruits of rectitude and wisdom. How unspeakably important, then, that this principle should be imbibed with the first lessons of our infancy and childhood, that it may grow with our growth and strengthen with our strength — that it may be permanently associated with the pure and hallowed influences of life's opening dawn, and serve as an amulet to protect us against the rudest assaults of the world and the strongest temptations to swerve from the path of duty! The responsibility in this respect, assumed by those to whom have been confided the task of furnishing the teachers of our elementary schools with the credentials of their high and holy office, can not be too seriously pondered.

Hitherto the question of the moral character of the teacher — the question which, above and beyond all others, is most important in its consequences—has been far too frequently postponed and neglected. The literary qualifications of the candidate have been seldom wholly overlooked—his capacity to instruct, to communicate knowledge to his pupils, and, above all, the price at which his services may be commanded, are scrutinized with the most jealous interest; but "the daily beauty of his life" is an element seldom entering into the account, and if no palpable stain rests upon his character, if his outward deportment conforms substantially to the standard recognized by the community at large, and he has hitherto come in conflict with none of its penal or social canons, he is regarded, if otherwise qualified, as abundantly competent to assume the guardianship of the elementary school. The result has been that, while the intellectual faculties of the pupil have been tasked frequently to their utmost tension, the moral virtues—those which alone can give a value and right direction to knowledge—those which alone can secure happiness and well-being—which alone can enable us adequately to fulfill all the duties appertaining to us as intelligent, social and responsible beings—have been neglected. The means of an indefinite progression in all that ennobles and dignifies our common humanity have been abundantly furnished; but their end and aim have not been communicated, and power to accomplish the most wonderful results has been conferred upon thousands without the most remote knowledge of the uses to which alone it can be efficiently consecrated.

The full and true idea of education can not be thoroughly realized until our elementary schools become the nurseries of our moral no less than of our intellectual and physical nature—until the mind is subjected from the period of its earliest development to that of its mature expansion to an enlightened and judicious cultivation of all its faculties—apprised of all its powers and their respective spheres of action—trained to a clear perception of intellectual and moral truths—imbued with an ardent love of excellence, and fortified and strengthened by a pervading sense of its own elevation, responsibility and destiny. The formation of such a character, and its multiplication and diffusion throughout the numerous thoroughfares of the social organization, would speedily elevate the condition of humanity in all its aspects and relations.

The great practical problem of the age in reference to education is in what way and by what means the intellectual and moral faculties of the young are to be so developed, cultivated and directed as to enable their possessors, at the earliest practicable period, to render them subservient to the varied purposes of existence. Accurately or even approximately to solve this difficult problem, demands all the energies of the clearest and most comprehensive intellect united to the most expansive philanthropy and to the most diversified experience of human nature. That a particular method of mental culture has in a given instance or a given number of instances been followed by a career of usefulness, honor and happiness, by no means authorizes us to conclude that a similar result will uniformly or even generally follow from a repetition of the process under other and different circumstances. So variously combined are the intellectual and moral powers in different individuals, so variously modified the elements of character by innumerable circumstances entering at every period of life into the mental structure, that it is next to impossible to lay down any fixed rule which shall enable the educator to mould aright in all cases the plastic energies of thought and action committed to his charge. More particularly is this remark applicable to the development and direction of the moral faculties. Motives and inducements which operate powerfully and irresistibly with one class of minds are found utterly impotent and inefficacious with another. Arguments and reasonings which address themselves at once to the comprehension and appreciation of one individual are urged in vain upon the understanding or the conscience of another. In some minds the convictions of the moral sense predominate over all the allurements of vicious inclinations, and in conjunction with a well-balanced intellect secure, apparently without effort, a course of conduct in accordance with the dictates of enlightened reason and Christian obligation, while in others so feebly compacted are the barriers of moral restraint, and so active and energetic the vicious propensities, that the entire tendency of the mental organization is reversed, and the attainment of confirmed habits of virtue rendered possible only by a painful, systematic and laborious process of self-culture, conducted under the most favorable auspices.

In short, the mental constitution and tendency of no two individuals of the race can be said to be the same, and consequently the elementary discipline which is to prepare them for the great arena of life, with its duties, responsibilities, struggles, reverses, triumphs, must be infinitely diversified in order to comprehend with any degree of ultimate success the innumerable varieties of disposition and temperament which are thus found to exist. Still it is by no means impracticable to arrive at certain fundamental principles which, if not universally applicable to the mental and moral discipline of youth, will in the great majority of instances enable the educator to give that direction to the opening mind which will best conduce to its subsequent development and expansion, to form those habits and mature those principles which are to constitute the future character, and to cultivate those virtues, the possession of which is so indispensable to happiness.

So important is a correct appreciation of these fundamental principles on the part of those who are charged with the education of the young, that it may safely be asserted that upon it depends almost exclusively the degree of success which their instructions, however valuable and comprehensive in an intellectual point of view, shall be found to have attained in the formation and development of character. Knowledge, however accurate and sound and firmly imbedded in the mind, is of no practical value to him whose moral nature has either been suffered to run to waste, or been distorted, disfigured and perverted by mistaken processes of discipline or the operation of untoward circumstances. By far the greater portion of the accumulated evils of our modern political and social organization are unquestionably attributable to the unequal development of the intellectual and moral faculties. The progress of mere knowledge, of scientific induction, of artistic skill and ingenuity, has outstripped the capacity, and not unfrequently even the disposition, to apply it to the highest and noblest purposes of life, and that power which was conferred upon man for the attainment of the perfection of his being in all its fair and beautiful proportions has been rendered subservient to mere material results of time and sense. The want of adaptation between the godlike faculties of thought and reason, creative and inventive power, combination and concentration of physical and mental effort, and the purposes in the civil, social and political economy, to which, with few exceptions, they have hitherto been applied, is mournfully apparent in the deranged structure of modern civilization. Vice and crime, suffering and misery, want and destitution, violence, rapine and bloodshed increase and multiply, with the increase and multiplication and diffusion of scientific knowledge and inventive skill, and the ponderous car of intellectual progress daily and hourly crushes beneath its remorseless wheels whole hecatombs of victims to the sordid selfishness, the cold indifference, or the unrestrained passions of our modern civilization.

This inequality in the advancement and improvement of the intellectual and moral faculties can be corrected only by a more equal and harmonious mental development and culture in early youth. Moral education should be contemporaneous and commensurate with the intellectual progress. The great ideas of duty and responsibility, of truth, virtue, simplicity and singleness of character, benevolence and beneficence, should be constantly and clearly kept in view, reflected from the perfect mirror of Christianity, and irradiated by the strong light of immortality. The atmosphere of the school-room should be perfectly free from the admixture of the baser ingredients of passion in any of their shapes or forms. The artless innocence of childhood should there uniformly find a congenial field for the realization of its joyous hopes, its beaming anticipations, its ardent desire for knowledge, for improvement and progress. The law of love, of kindness, of disinterested regard for the welfare and happiness of others, of sympathy for their woes, of forgiveness and forgetfulness of injuries, should be enforced by all those considerations derived from the natural and moral world which are constantly present to the eye and to the mind, and not an incident capable of being seized upon without the appearance of an effort, and affording an apt illustration of some valuable moral lesson, should be suffered to pass unimproved.

Mildness and dignity of demeanor on the part of the teacher, perfect self-possession and perfect freedom from affectation, accompanied by the uniform manifestation of a paternal regard for the true interests, welfare and happiness of each individual committed to his charge, will seldom fail to make a deep and indelible impression upon the ingenuous moral nature of those who daily witness these attractive exhibitions. The cardinal elements of conduct and character thus insensibly become interfused and incorporated with their intellects and hearts, and under the fostering influences of paternal and social co-operation will speedily ripen into durable habits and fixed principles of goodness and virtue. The occasional or frequent exhibition of passion, whether it assume the form of irritability, peevishness, harshness of expression, inequality of temper or corporal inflictions, is wholly repugnant to every sound theory or enlightened conception of intellectual or moral education. If, as the advocates for the retention of physical punishment in our elementary institutions of learning contend, the interests of education in its most comprehensive sense, including the development of the intellectual as well as the moral nature, are in truth promoted by these means, a phenomenon would be presented strikingly at variance with the ordinary results of mental philosophy as deduced from the most comprehensive and thorough examination of humanity in all its recognized elements. If by the infliction of stripes, by corporal chastisement other than such as may be designed to effect needful restraint from the perpetuation of evil or of mischief, or to secure obedience to the reasonable requisitions of the teacher, the intellectual powers are developed or strengthened, or the moral faculties cultivated and expanded, a new and distinct element of knowledge exists not heretofore enumerated by philosophers or educationists—an element, too, which is always at hand, and one but too congenial to a certain class of minds, which, unfortunately for the interests of education, has long exercised an important influence over the details of elementary public instruction. The ablest writers on educational topics, both in Europe and America, not only of the present day but from the earliest period of modern civilization—practical and experienced teachers, whose success in the communication of knowledge and the formation of character has been most abundant and satisfactory—and by far the greater portion of those who in an official capacity have been called upon to superintend this extensive department of our political and social economy, have concurred in the uniform and repeated expression of the inadequacy, inexpediency and injurious tendency of this mode of discipline. So powerful, universal and strong has been the manifestation of an enlightened public opinion in this respect, that while in nine out of ten, and perhaps a still larger proportion, of the public schools of Germany, France and Holland, and in all those institutions which we have during nearly a quarter of a century regarded as the most perfect models, this species of punishment has entirely disappeared, in our own schools it has been driven to the very utmost verge of toleration, and is with gratifying unanimity recognized only as the "forlorn hope," the ultimate resort when all other means of discipline have been faithfully and perseveringly attempted and failed.

Wherever teachers have been found possessing the requisite talents and administrative ability to secure the pleasing exercise of the intellectual and moral faculties upon the innumerable objects of nature and art—to call into play the finer and nobler sentiments of the affections—so to vary the routine of instruction as to afford room for the equal and harmonious development of the characteristic germs of intellect and of thought which are found to exist in each, and to substitute the universal sanctions of morality, which the most immature intellect can comprehend and appreciate, for the summary appeal to force and violence, the results have uniformly been such as triumphantly to vindicate the principle here asserted. The path of knowledge becomes strewed with flowers; the virtues and graces of humanity bud, blossom and expand under the genial influences of kindness and love, and the foundations of future usefulness, happiness and well-being are permanently and durably laid. The teacher comes to his task with a mind thoroughly imbued with the principles and details of elementary knowledge—in full possession of physical health—with a firm determination to refrain from every, the least, exhibition of passion or of temper—with an amiable disposition and a heart "open as day" to all the mild and holy and beautiful influences of childhood. By an indefinable attraction, which experience has shown to be almost as invariable and as certain as that of the magnet to the pole, the hearts of the children intuitively respond to these unaffected manifestations of interest and regard which beam from the countenance and pervade the actions of a teacher thus mentally constituted. At a suitable hour the buoyant energies of the tumultuous and busy crowd are temporarily checked, and a strain of music, attuned to sweetest harmony, even in the midst of apparent discord, by innocent and happy voices, insensibly but effectually soothes, solemnizes and elevates the mind, and prepares it to listen reverently and with attention to the words of Him who "spake as never man spake," and to unite with their teacher in ascription of thanksgiving to the great Governor of the universe for all his blessings, and the expression of filial trust in him for their continuance.

This periodical and solemn recognition of the

relations which exist between the Creator of the universe and themselves can not fail to exert a most beneficial influence upon the minds and the consciences of the children, and to impress them with a sense of moral responsibility eminently favorable to the development of their mental faculties. The pupils are then distributed, arranged and grouped together into classes according to their respective attainments and proficiency, and page after page of the varied and ample volume of knowledge is unfolded to their view—its contents clearly and methodically pointed out and explained, their connection with the world of matter and of mind demonstrated and applied, and the desire for progressive advancement induced and strengthened by each succeeding step. When the physical and mental energies of the pupils begin to flag, the equilibrium is restored by changing the order of exercises—by the inspiriting effects of music, or by the refreshing influences of muscular exercises in the open air.

Occasional symptoms of insubordination—the involuntary recurrence perhaps of habits not yet entirely extirpated—the results it may be of incipient physical derangement or of mental discomfort—of an irrepressible propensity for the time being to escape from the salutary control of authority, however lightly it may press, or of heedlessness and thoughtlessness—in short, any of those multifarious and often inexplicable sources of perverted action which seem to be the heritage of humanity in its best estate, are met by a direct or indirect appeal to the supremacy of the nobler reason, to the controlling and restraining force of the higher faculties of thought and action, or successfully repelled by a skillful diversion of the mental and corporal energies to some more attractive field of exercise. Affectionate and well-timed appeals to the moral sense and better feelings of the more serious offender, accompanied if necessary by the indirect but powerful pressure of adequate restraint within certain specific boundaries beyond which transgression is rendered impracticable—these, together with a variety of efficient motives which may be brought to bear by a skillful and experienced teacher, speedily put an end to the offense, while they at the same time effectually reprove the offender. Sentiments of reciprocal affection and attached regard insensibly spring up between the teacher and each individual under his charge, and the atmosphere of the school-room soon becomes so congenial to the child that he looks forward to the hours devoted to its pleasing exercises and grateful recreations both of body and of mind with joyful anticipations and an indescribable pleasure. Then come the exhilarating excitement and enjoyment of the periodical examinations, exhibitions and celebrations; the eager but chastened competition; the desire of excellence and the struggle for success; the tumultuous but interesting throng of happy faces and beating hearts; and the triumphant exhibition of useful acquisitions; thus agreeably fixing forever in their memories and hearts the joyous associations of the school, unaccompanied by the festering recollection of scenes of violence, passion, vindictiveness, cruelty or harshness.

CHAPTER XII.

SUPERVISION AND INSPECTION.

THE experience of the most enlightened educators of our own and other countries, and the concurring testimony of all writers on this topic, coincide in placing the influences exerted on our institutions of elementary public instruction by frequent visitation and thorough inspection at the head of the most efficient means for their advancement and improvement. To these more than to any other source, or to all other sources combined, are to be attributed the superior excellence and comparative perfection of the schools of Prussia, Germany and Holland. Deprived of these, the most varied and profound attainments on the part of the teacher, the most judicious system of culture and discipline, and the most liberal public or private appropriations in aid of popular education will not accomplish the great object which all should have in view. The invigorating effects of a faithful and systematic supervision alone can maintain that pervading sense of responsibility on the part of the teacher, and that consciousness of a sympathetic interest, beyond the limit of the school-room, on the part of the pupils, which furnish the aliment and the excitement to the labors of both.

The superintendent or inspector is presumed to be in all essential respects well versed in the science of education; to be master of its principles as well comprehensively as in detail; to be conversant with the best and most approved modes of instruction, of government and of discipline; to be acquainted with the practical operation and result of different systems of mental culture, and capable of distinguishing between such as are, upon the whole, best adapted to the purposes in view, and such as are defective in principle and untenable theory, in discriminating between the systems themselves and their administration; of judiciously separating what is unsound and impracticable in each from what, in itself and when properly administered, is valuable and worthy of adoption; and of so combining the varied excellences of all, while he rejects every admixture of error, as to secure and perpetuate a firm basis upon which future improvements may be superinduced. The frequent presence, advice and counsel of such an officer can not fail of exerting a marked influence on the progress of the school. The information which he is able to communicate respecting the condition of other schools in the town and in the country; the encouraging assurances which he gives of the interest manifested in every section of the state—in adjoining states, in Europe—on the subject of that great system of elementary public instruction, of which the humblest and most obscure school forms a part; the improvements which he suggests, the inducements he holds out, the hopes he encourages, and the enthusiasm he imparts to teacher, to parents and to pupils—all these motive powers to enlightened and persevering effort in the attainment and diffusion of knowledge are eminently conducive to the steady advancement and rapid improvement of our common schools. Without these, swarms of mere pedagogues—vapid pretenders to knowledge, lifeless drones expelled from every other department of industry for their unfitness and want of capacity—will find a safe and unquestioned retreat where they should most vigilantly be excluded, where they can not fail of accomplishing the most disastrous results, where they poison the very fountains of knowledge and character and happiness, and sow in profusion those seeds of idleness, of ignorance and of vice which no after-culture can effectually eradicate. Without these, the most impracticable and absurd systems of mis-called instruction are perpetuated—a monotonous and unintelligible routine of dull formalities is repeated for days and weeks and months without the communication of a single idea, or the inculcation of a solitary principle of virtue—the bodies and the minds of the unhappy victims of ignorance and credulity are oppressed and perverted, and the season of youth and innocence and enjoyment—the period when, under more genial and enlightened auspices, the glorious light of the sun and the inspiring breezes of heaven are not more welcome to the buoyant energies of the physical nature than are knowledge and instruction to the mind—this brief and beautiful spring-time of life—so brief, so evanescent, and yet so rich with the germs of future progress and expansion—becomes the darkest, the most hopeless and most gloomy period of existence. The history of the past in this respect abundantly confirms the accuracy of the picture here drawn.

The government and discipline of the schools, including the mode of teaching pursued, constitute an essential feature in their character and means of usefulness, and should be faithfully and thoroughly scrutinized. In the absence of a systematic preparation of teachers, through the agency of a seminary expressly devoted to this purpose, the officers called upon to investigate their qualifications can of necessity look no farther than their general moral character and intellectual attainments. They possess no means of knowing their capability of communicating instruction to others, even in those branches in which they are themselves most thoroughly conversant and familiar. They can not penetrate behind the veil of that external moral deportment which may nevertheless conceal deplorable inequalities of temper, uncongeniality of spirit with the vocation of the teacher, and a total want of affinity to the nature of youthful minds — a nature sure to be attracted, as the needle to the pole, toward the magnet of a congenial mind. They must see the teacher in the school-room—ascertain his practical qualifications for the discharge of the duties which he has undertaken — his views of the science of education and the practical result of those views — his mode of developing the intellectual faculties and cultivating the moral nature of his pupils under the diversified manifestations of each, which are constantly presented to his notice

— his system of government and discipline, and its effects; and they must critically observe from time to time the progress which, under his direction, his pupils have made — not in knowledge merely, but in that sound mental and moral culture which forms and matures *character.*

Under the vast impulse which has been given to the philosophy of the human mind during the last half-century, elementary education has assumed the rank, and, we may almost add, the precision and certainty of a science. Its principles have been thoroughly investigated by the ablest and most profound minds, and all its details have been subjected to the test of practical analysis under circumstances well adapted to the ascertainment of truth. The teacher, therefore, who feels the dignity and importance of his profession, and earnestly desires to discharge his whole duty, has it in his power to familiarize himself with the results of the experience of those who, in his own and other countries, have sought out and applied the best methods of instruction and discipline, and he owes it to himself, as well as to his employers and the community, to attain and avail himself of this knowledge to the utmost practical extent. His system of instruction should be in accordance with the soundest principles of educational science — adapted to the moral and intellectual requirements of every grade of mind—eminently practical in all its departments—and so administered as to carry forward the mental faculties of each and every pupil to the attainment in the shortest possible period of that power of self-culture and self-control which shall enable him, in every emergency of life, to "act well his part," and fulfill the various duties appertaining to him as a moral and intelligent being. If the teacher is radically deficient in these high requisites of his calling—if he lacks practical efficiency—if he is wanting in that aptitude in the communication of instruction without which the highest degree of learning is of no avail beyond the precincts of his own mind —above all, if he manifests no interest in his vocation, no sympathy with the expanding minds around him, no enlightened appreciation of the interests committed to his charge, and no capability of drawing forth and developing the immortal germ of mind in the rich and various soil spread out before him—he should be frankly and fully advised of his deficiency, and promptly removed from a station where his longer continuance must be productive of unmitigated evil—the consequences of which, immediate and remote, are and must be, from the nature of the case, incalculable. It must be borne in mind that our schools are designed for the benefit, not of the teacher, but of the pupils, and that the interests of the latter should be made invariably to take precedence of the former, whenever the two come in conflict.

CHAPTER XIII.

SYSTEMS OF PUBLIC INSTRUCTION — THEIR ERRORS AND DEFECTS.

IT is customary on public occasions to indulge somewhat indiscriminately in laudatory encomiums on the progress and advancement of popular education; to felicitate ourselves on the assurance that the period in which we live has attained to the perfection of human excellence and power; that the country of our birth or adoption, the institutions we and our forefathers have built up, the high civilization which surrounds us, the rich treasures of our past history, and the bright prospects which await us in the future are unsurpassed in the annals of recorded time. It may be that the essential spirit of these complacent allegations is to a very considerable extent justified by the incontrovertible facts which surround us as a people. It is, however, the part of wisdom from time to time to inquire, with all due reverence and humility, whether the most decided superiority of attainment and advancement implies excellence of the highest practicable grade — whether, rapid and brilliant as has been our progress in literary and scientific culture, much does not yet remain to be effected — many prejudices and errors to be overcome, many improvements to be made, and whether it may not be expedient occasionally to pause in our onward career, calmly and dispassionately to review our position and ascertain its permanent lights and shades, its true tendencies, and the sources alike of its weakness and its strength.

It may be said, the time has not yet come when we may safely discard the authority of long established usage, even though that usage be clearly demonstrated to be untenable in principle, and unsatisfactory, if not pernicious, in its results. We are surrounded on every hand by institutions, habits, usages, principles, many of them originating in past centuries, under the influence of agencies whose forces have long since ceased to operate, some of them wholly indefensible in theory and injurious in practice, and others simply barren and obsolete, which, nevertheless, we continue to retain and cherish by general consent, while they are manifestly retarding our intellectual progress, undermining the very fabric of our moral being, and eating, like a canker, at the sources of our individual prosperity and happiness. Rash innovations are doubtless to be deprecated, in every department of our political, social, or personal relations; but of what avail are advancing knowledge and the accumulated experience of ages, if we neglect to apply them, as they are attained, to the removal of existing abuses, the dissipation of erroneous theories, the abandonment of false principles and the substitution of sound views of life and action?

With every allowance for that salutary distrust of the entire accuracy of our own strongest convictions, which would preclude us from immediate and efficient action in the direction to which they may point, we may, at least, submit these convictions, in all their force, to the candid and dispassionate consideration of our fellow-men, and to the unbiased judgment of those who are to succeed us on life's busy stage—of those whose minds and hearts are yet comparatively free from the hardening or the debilitating influences of the world, and whose interest in the practical recognition of truth and duty is, as yet, unaffected by the almost irresistible pressure of conflicting circumstances. When, therefore, we venture to arraign before the general bar of that public sentiment which may truly be characterized as "the heir of all the ages, in the foremost files of time," any of the shortcomings, faults or foibles of our educational systems, it is not with any claim to infallibility in the convictions we have reached, or any expectation or desire of effecting an immediate and radical change; but simply and solely with the design of remitting them for a fair and impartial trial before a competent tribunal, that their character and results may be fully investigated and a true verdict rendered accordingly.

First, then, our systems of popular education and public instruction, taken as a whole, do not seem to be sufficiently *comprehensive*, either in their aim or their results. They do not adequately provide for the physical, intellectual, moral and spiritual wants of our nature. They do not adequately fit us for the varied duties, cares and responsibilities of active life. They fail to confer upon us the power of self-culture by the timely, harmonious and judicious development of *all* the faculties of our being. They regard the subjects of their discipline too much as classes, and too little as individuals. They take cognizance too exclusively of the intellectual, to the neglect of the moral and religious nature, the affections and the heart. They have regard rather to attainments than conduct—to knowledge than character—to the flower than to the fruit. And second, as systems they are fragmentary, disconnected, incomplete, and consequently comparatively inefficient. The elementary or common school is found in great perfection in many portions of our country, but completely isolated from the higher institutions of learning. Academies, colleges and universities are scattered over the land, each occupying an independent position, and having no connection with those above or below them in the scale of literary advancement. No effective provision is made for the intellectual and moral culture of large and rapidly increasing classes of children and adults, who are thus left a prey to the grossest ignorance and the most formidable temptations to crime.

Not only the power but the obligation of the State to provide ample facilities for the education of all its future citizens, is fully conceded by modern legislators and statesmen, and throughout New England, in New York, Pennsylvania, many of the Western and some of the Southern States this great principle is recognized, and to a greater or less extent carried out by statutory enactments. But whence is this power derived, and out of what circumstances does the obligation spring? Both are clearly derived from the reciprocal rights and duties of the governing and the governed—the one affording protection to persons and property, securing peace and order and upholding the majesty and the supremacy of the laws, and the other submitting to all necessary and proper restraints, and yielding up a portion of their natural liberty for the attainment of these high and most desirable purposes. Neither of these objects can be accomplished, save under an iron despotism, in the absence of general intelligence. Every citizen, therefore, possesses an indefeasible right to the free acquisition of knowledge, of which no government has the right to deprive him; and it is not only the duty but the highest interest of every republican government, regarded in a merely political point of view, to provide for the widest possible diffusion of knowledge. But while every citizen may thus demand of the government the provision of all the requisite facilities for a liberal education, why may not the government, with equal propriety, demand of every citizen that he shall faithfully avail himself of these facilities, when thus furnished for his own mental and moral culture, and that of those placed under his charge? Is it not notorious that the millions and hundreds of millions lavished with such profuse and bounteous liberality for the education of the people during the past half-century have been rendered almost nugatory, so far as the criminal expenses of governments are concerned, by the continued prevalence of those large masses of ignorance, combined with destitution and vagabondism, which are found in all our great cities and towns, and infest, to an alarmingly increasing extent, even the quietude and seclusion of our rural villages and hamlets? Would it not be wise to arrest this fearfully downward tendency by the efficient exertion of that unquestionable power which every commonwealth possesses, not only to furnish abundant facilities for the education of all its future citizens, but to insist that each and every one of those citizens shall, in some way and to such an extent at least as may afford reasonable assurances of upright and virtuous conduct, participate in these advantages? Can any system of popular education and public instruction, however skillfully devised and ably administered, hope permanently to elevate the condition and advance the progress of individuals and communities while hemmed in and surrounded on every hand by the impenetrable legions of ignorance and crime?

The time has arrived when with us education should not only be universal but practical, thorough and comprehensive. It is not enough that a portion merely, however large, or even the majority of the people should participate in its benefits. *Every individual*, however obscure, friendless, destitute, vicious or imbecile, should be taken by the hand at the earliest dawn of his faculties, and trained to habits and principles of virtue, his intellect enlightened and expanded, and all the various faculties of his nature harmoniously developed and directed. It is not enough that the elementary principles of science should be communicated to the rising generation. Liberal provision should be made for the most advanced culture which the necessities or the inclinations of the individual mind may require, and the extent and degree of that culture should be limited only by those circumstances and tendencies which clearly prescribe the future course of life and theatre of action of each. In other words, each individual should be assured such an amount and degree of literary, scientific and artistical knowledge as he may deem necessary or desirable for all those objects, ends and aims which his peculiar situation in life, his predominant tastes, genius, ambition and powers specially require. Then, and then only, will he be fully qualified to discharge all the duties incumbent upon him, and to reimburse to the community a thousand-fold the amount it has thus wisely and generously expended in his education. By this liberal policy, and by this alone, will the State assure itself of the consecration to its highest interests, moral, social, political and material, of all the faculties, energies, and powers of each one of its citizens, afford free scope for the legitimate and pleasurable exercise of every mental endowment, circumscribe within the smallest limits the domain of vice and crime, pauperism and destitution, by conferring upon all the ability, and with it, so far as may be attainable in the present imperfect condition of humanity, the inclination to pursue a career of usefulness, honor, fame and virtue. I am not enthusiast enough to suppose, indeed, that by any possible advancement of society or education the wayward passions of our frail and perverted nature in their myriad combinations, with infinitely varying circumstances and conditions, often hopelessly struggling under a heavy burden of transmitted and powerful propensities to evil, can be so disciplined and trained as to render the criminal tribunal and the detective police, the prison, the penitentiary and the gallows, the poor-house, the hospital and the asylum, the discarded relics of a past age. But when I am solemnly assured by the ablest, most experienced, intelligent, and upright educators of the age, speaking without concert, with entire unanimity and the most perfect confidence, that, with only the limited and imperfect means now possessed by them and their associates for the education of the rising generation, ninety-nine out of every hundred committed to their charge during the period ordinarily devoted to elementary instruction, may be made the ornaments and the pride of society—virtuous, intelligent and useful men, good citizens, truthful witnesses, enlightened and impartial judges and jurors—prompt to every good work and to every noble impulse of humanity, and fully prepared for the discharge of every duty and obligation of life; when, too, from personal and careful investigation of the records of criminal conviction of the most populous state in the Union, during a period of ten consecutive years, I find that of nearly thirty thousand convicts, less than three hundred had received such an education as the best country schools now afford; when I look into our immense and costly establishments for the support and maintenance of thé poor, and find them almost exclusively occupied by the grossly ignorant and uneducated, not one in a thousand with any pretensions to literary culture—when I deliberately weigh and compare and reflect upon these results, they seem to me abundantly to justify the most sanguine anticipations for the future well-being of society and of individuals, as the direct consequence of universal, wise and well-directed moral and intellectual culture.

In order, however, to secure to the greatest possible extent the blessings of a sound and universal education, there must exist a systematic-enlightened co-operation between different grades of institutions. The primary or purely elementary school, the grammar school, the high school, the academy, the college and the university must constitute parts of one great and comprehensive system, each aiming at specific results, with direct and constant reference both to that by which it is preceded and to that which is to follow it, and all combined constituting a full and complete course of instruction with reference, to the greatest practicable extent, to the particular wants and probable future destination of each of its subjects. The State has already taken under its especial patronage and regard the common school in all its various departments; in some instances it has even gone farther, and made liberal provisions for a higher academical, and in one instance, at least — that of the New York Free College—for a complete collegiate course. Why should it not expand its arms and embrace within its beneficent scope every grade of instruction, from the lowest to the highest, from the infant or primary school to the university — calling to its aid every variety of talent and ability which the country affords, and presenting a powerful and efficient stimulus to the utmost exertion and highest skill of the most accomplished scholars and the most finished education?

Of all these institutions, the lowest in rank—the primary or elementary school—is far the most important. It is there that the foundations of future character are, or should be, laid; there that a permanent and abiding impulse is or should be given to the intellect, the affections, and the will. It is a great mistake to suppose that the work of education does not commence until the intellect is sufficiently matured fully to comprehend the propositions laid before it. From the earliest dawn of sensation, from the first faint impressions of the external world, throughout the entire period of infancy, the work of education, intellectually and morally, is in active and incessant progress, and far greater and more astonishing advances are made than at any subsequent period. The earlier, therefore, after this period, the child is committed to the charge of a competent instructor, the better. Instead, however, of that senseless, tedious and monotonous routine of letters, syllables, words and phrases which so generally occupies the hours devoted to elementary instruction, the first years of school life should be exclusively occupied in what has been so beautifully and expressively characterized by an eloquent writer and eminently practical educator of New England as "Unconscious Tuition"—in the gentle development and training of the affections; in the discipline of the passions, at that only period when they can be effectually disciplined; in the communication of a general knowledge of the productions of nature, and the various combinations of art; in the delightful culture of the imagination—that important faculty which takes such marvelous possession of the infant mind, that wonderful depository where are gathered up, in life's bright and sunny morning, those inexhaustible treasures of transfigured Nature, to be reproduced, in future days, with all their cherished associations, as the living poetry of existence, the prolonged memory of life's fresh and fragrant dawn—

"Those first affections,
Those shadowy recollections,
Which, be they what they may,
Are yet the fountain-light of all our day,
Are yet a master-light of all our seeing,
Uphold us, cherish us, and have power to make
Our noisy years seem moments in the being
Of the eternal silence, truths that wake
To perish never,
Which neither listlessness nor mad endeavor,
Nor man, nor boy,
Nor all that is at enmity with joy,
Can utterly abolish, or destroy."

It is here, in the primary school, that childhood, surrounded by all the pleasant associations of home affections, familiarized with the beautiful in nature and in art, all its energies of thought and action agreeably stimulated and excited, and all its impulses pure, unselfish, and innocent, should be gently and unconsciously moulded into every form of mental and moral excellence and power. If this decisive period be suffered to pass by without improvement—if these rapidly-fleeting hours have flown onward without gathering and assimilating those amaranthine flowers of beauty, virtue, truthfulness and love, which shed their fragrance over the whole of life's future path, there is slender probability that at any subsequent period the golden opportunity can be recalled. The associations connected with childhood are, as we all know, intimately bound up with the principles, habits, pursuits and aspirations of manhood—entering as an essential element into the very web and woof of character — unconsciously stealing into the "chambers of imagination," and asserting their power amid the strongest temptations and in the hour of deepest trial. They constitute a reserved fund of moral and spiritual strength to be drawn upon when every other source may perchance have failed — a life-boat in which the wrecked outcast of humanity may safely reach the haven of rest.

The cultivation of the intellect follows, naturally and gracefully, in the train of this genial and kindly discipline of the moral and spiritual nature in its earliest expansion; and from this point the two should be inseparable. In the normal and healthful condition of the affections —the just and equal balance of the moral nature —the mental powers instinctively demand knowledge from every attainable source. Knowledge, first of all, of the wonderful world in which they are placed; of the external universe in all its departments; of sensible and material objects—their origin, uses and ends; next, of the human race; the history of mankind; the annals of states, empires, kingdoms and governments; the biography and remarkable traits of eminent, good and great men; then, of the more abstruse and higher departments of science; the structure and philosophy of language; the complex and yet simple combinations of mathematical demonstration; the sublime teachings of astronomy; the vast and almost inconceivable periods and hieroglyphical records of geology; the varied combinations and transformations of chemistry; the mysteries of electricity, magnetism, and their kindred powers; until they reach those deeper and profounder mysteries of the human soul itself—its origin, its powers, its varied capacities of enjoyment and suffering, and its immortality.

And here, as it seems to me—in this department of intellectual training—our existing systems of education far too generally fall short of that practical efficiency, that breadth and depth and comprehensiveness of culture, which is alike demanded by the structure and requirements of the human mind, and by the varied and pressing wants of society There is too much of didactic and authoritative teaching, too little of inductive and suggestive; too much of instruction, and too little of that higher and better education which confers substantial and permanent power — the power of self-culture—the independent, free, bold and invigorating exercise of one's own individual faculties. The elementary principles of every science, the foundations upon which it rests, its alphabet, its essential structure and components, its symbols and terminology, must, indeed, be communicated; and in all these respects the utmost accuracy, precision, fullness and clearness of enunciation and illustration are indispensable. Beyond this the student should be thrown as much as possible upon his own resources, and left to follow out these fundamental principles to their legitimate conclusions on the pinions of his own expanding intellect, aided only, and that sparingly, when his utmost energies have been faithfully but unavailingly put forth to reach some necessary but otherwise unattainable height.

The habit of close, continuous, accurate induction—of analyzing principles and tracing them to their conclusions—of sounding the depths of scientific investigation—of detecting and removing fallacies—rejecting erroneous preconceptions and prejudices, and examining questions from every attainable point of view and on every side, before definitively passing upon them — is, of itself, a most valuable discipline of the mental powers, essential, indeed, to the formation of a sound thinker and practical reasoner. How often, in the intercourse of society, in the transaction of its most important and momentous affairs, in the halls of legislation, the tribunal of justice, the haunts of commerce, the pulpit and the press, the numerous literary and scientific associations of the day, at the polls, do we feel and lament the absence of this great element of accurate, impartial, discriminating judgment—unbiased by passion, unfettered by prejudice, untrammeled by authority, accessible to conviction, open to truth, from whatsoever source it may present itself, and suspending its verdict whenever facts or circumstances material to the integrity of its deliverance are wanting! How many questions of political economy, legal interpretation, polemical casuistry, social improvement and advancement, and national policy, as well as of facts and phenomena of deep scientific import, are left open and unsettled from age to age, to be renewedly agitated and discussed by each successive generation, for want of the infusion into the arguments by which they are supported or denied of clear conceptions, sound inductions and just conclusions.

As one of the numerous illustrations which might be adduced of this practical inability or indisposition to fathom to the depths questions, even of general interest and importance, the past history and the present condition of the alleged science of phrenology may be cited. If the pretensions of that science are founded on truth—based upon a sound, exhaustive and comprehensive induction of facts, and capable of practical application in the formation or interpretation of character and its results in the actual conduct of life—then it should be assigned a prominent place, not only in the philosophy of the human mind, but in the education of the rising generation. If, on the other hand, its premises are false, its reasonings inconsequential and its conclusions baseless, uncertain, vague and valueless for all practical purposes, its principles and theories should be promptly and authoritatively consigned to the same oblivion which has long entombed the ancient cabala of judicial astrology. Now the most abundant materials have long existed for the definite solution of this problem on clear and incontrovertible grounds. While, on the one hand, it is systematically and almost universally excluded from every course of instruction, on the other, its fundamental principles find a deep and permanent though perhaps unacknowledged lodgment in many of the ripest intellects and acutest reasoners of the age. Many of the most eminent educationists of Europe and America, many of the most distinguished professional men in every department of active life have practically governed themselves by its teachings and shaped their instructions by its theories, without professedly incorporating them into their intellectual and moral discipline, or proposing their adoption as an elementary portion of the text-books of their science. Not only the highest interests of education, but the general welfare of humanity, the advancement of science, as well as the culture of the heart and the management of the life, sound philosophy as well as true religion, demand the definitive settlement of this long-pending question, and in a manner satisfactory and conclusive to the humblest equally with the most enlightened understandings. So with a great variety of other theories, equally important and equally undetermined: the morality and expediency of slavery; the principles of free trade or a protective tariff; the fundamental questions of political economy; the true functions and proper limits of government; the relation and connection of Church and State; religious toleration; freedom of speech and of the press; and, in short, all those religious, moral, political and social speculations which float from century to century and from age to age down the tide of time, to be continually transmitted, with increased intricacy and embarrassment, from generation to generation. The human intellect is so constituted that a proper cultivation of its various faculties might unquestionably enable it to bring to bear upon all these subjects the clear light of demonstrative truth, whether originating in its own exhaustive reasonings, or reflected, with a full appreciation of its successive processes and results, from the operation of other minds. In all ages and at all times, the intellectual guides of humanity, "the crowned kings of thought," each from his own Olympian hill, have harmoniously responded to the utterance of those oracular truths, the practical application of which, to the most complicated problems of life, unlooses the "Gordian knots" of sophistry and error. It needs only that the mass of mind occupying the plains and the valleys, the highways and the by-ways of the world, be equally enlightened and disciplined to avail itself of its birthright, and like a giant awakening from its long slumber, shake off the mental and moral incubus which has so long weighed down its mighty energies.

It has also not unfrequently been observed, although this may seem to conflict in some measure with the suggestions in which I have already indulged, that too large a proportion of the time usually appropriated to intellectual instruction is devoted to the purely elementary branches of study, to the exclusion of their practical applications in the more advanced courses. The fundamental principles and essential rules of English Grammar, Arithmetic, Algebra and Geometry may, I feel confident, under a proper and judicious course of instruction, be thoroughly mastered by any pupil of ordinary intelligence and comprehension, in a much shorter period than that usually required in our public schools; and the time now, as I conceive, unprofitably expended in going over the same ground from time to time, in the form of reviews, or additional illustrations of the same principles slightly varied in form, might, perhaps, be better improved by transferring the illustrations and applications of the principles already fixed in the mind to a higher range of subjects requiring new combinations of thought, and bringing into action other faculties and powers of the intellect. This consideration derives additional force from the multiplicity of sciences now pressing upon the attention of the student, compared with the restricted range which formerly existed, rendering too protracted a devotion to the minute details of each, inconsistent with that clearly defined and practical acquaintance with all, which the demands of the age imperatively require.

Instances are by no means rare, in almost every community, of creditable and praiseworthy endowments in the mathematics and English Grammar and their cognate branches, without the slightest ability to carry out their principles to any of the ordinary purposes of life—without any intelligent conception of the great "well of English, undefiled," embodied in the noble creations of modern literature—of the treasures of art and science by which we, of the present age, are surrounded—of the monitory lessons of ancient and modern history—or even of the government and institutions of the country in which we dwell. That time which should have been spent in attaining a general and familiar acquaintance with the entire range of the sciences, bestowing on each only that amount and degree of labor and study requisite to its clear understanding, and passing on in succession to the conquest and occupancy of more advanced ground, has been injudiciously monopolized by a portion only of those elementary branches which, however essential in themselves as constituent parts of a full course, are of little or no value independently of that course. That which might have been the highest wisdom in the middle of the last century, or even at the commencement of the present, becomes utterly inapplicable to the changed condition of literary and scientific knowledge at the present day.

In the higher institutions of learning, also, a more generous and practical course of instruction seems to be demanded by the exigencies of the age and the rapid advancement of knowledge. These institutions, not to any considerable extent participating in the guidance or patronage of the State, and laboring under the many disadvantages and embarrassments inseparable from private or corporate management—fettered by restrictions and usages, and cramped by forms and precedents derived from past ages—are comparatively unaffected by that outside pressure of public sentiment and those urgent requirements of progressive civilization which are so constantly brought to bear upon the more elementary agencies of popular education. They are eminently conservative in their spirit, but conservative, it is greatly to be apprehended, together with those prominent features that constitute their high claims to the public confidence and regard, of much that is worthless and obsolete, if not absolutely pernicious. Too disproportionate a share of the brief period allotted to the course of instruction is devoted to purely mathematical culture and the study of the ancient languages—too little time is given to the mastery and application of those extensive branches of modern science, literature and art, which "come home to the business and the bosoms" of the world of the nineteenth century. Ample scope should doubtless be afforded to both, and neither should be passed over superficially or empirically.

To remedy these defects, universities, in fact as well as in name, should be organized and liberalty endowed at each great centre of scholastic resort—professorships of each distinct department of learning established and maintained, and every facility afforded for the acquirement of a complete and finished education, adapted to the specific wants and future destination of each pupil. These institutions, as I have already intimated, should be provided and efficiently sustained by the State, and placed under the general and special supervision of its ablest and most enlightened citizens. What nobler or higher function has the State than such a preparation of its future citizens for extended usefulness, for scientific discovery and research, for literary and artistic excellence, for the indefinite enhancement and diffusion of material wealth, for the prosecution of those great enterprises which enrich and aggrandize communities and nations, for the perpetuation of peace and concord at home and abroad, for the dispersion of ignorance, error, pauperism and crime, and the prevalence of knowledge, justice and Christianity?

The great and leading object of all true education is to prepare its recipient for a life of usefulness, integrity, honor and happiness here, and for the higher scenes and associations which await him in that unending future to which all our hopes and aspirations tend. To this end we store the mind with varied knowledge, that it may comprehend all those instrumentalities and agencies which may be brought to bear upon the pursuits of life—that it may take cognizance of its own mysterious and unfathomable nature, and exert its various and wonderful faculties, each in its own appropriate sphere, for the advancement of its own well-being, and the benefit and welfare of those within the circle of its influence—that it may avail itself of the ample experience of the past, through the thoughts, actions, trials and sufferings of the great, the wise and the good, as well as of the erring, the guilty and the criminal —that it may gather to itself, and assimilate and appropriate to its own individual being, all that the external universe has of beauty, sublimity, magnificence and harmony—all that the human mind has uttered of grandeur, melody, wisdom and power—all that human art has moulded into imperishable forms of loveliness and grace—all that science in its spacious domains has to bestow —all that the passing incidents of the busy world, in their manifold combinations of the "still, sad music of humanity," have to teach. To this end we cultivate the spiritual and immortal nature, that it may know its origin, worship and adore its great Creator, learn his will, bow to his behests, trust in his goodness, confide in his assurances of mercy and love, reverently and believingly accept his revelations of himself to humanity, "do justly, love mercy, and walk humbly before God." Have our institutions of learning, our common schools, academies, colleges and universities as yet been enabled adequately to realize in their various courses of instruction, in their bountiful provisions for the intellectual and moral culture of the young, these great and essential ideals? Has it been—is it now—their ambition, their end, their aim, their "exceeding great reward," to educate their pupils for eternity—to imbue them in the early spring-time of their existence, while their minds and hearts are yet open to every impression, with the spirit and the precepts of Christianity, to form their characters, mature their principles, confirm their habits, and direct their conduct in accordance with the dictates of that wisdom which "cometh from above," and which alone can guide us and them safely and unharmed through the countless perils of "this present evil world?" Are they preparing for the broad arena of human life—with its multifarious and diversified interests—men and women who shall go forth to adorn its various walks, to add to the sum of human happiness and contract the circle of human misery, and to diffuse around them on every hand the knowledge and genial elements of goodness and virtue and truth and love? Or are they sending forth mere scholars, with varied mental accomplishments, but destitute alike of practical skill and that high moral and spiritual culture which are indispensable to true worth and greatness? Do they so discipline the intellectual faculties of their pupils as to enable them, from their own resources, to separate the pure gold of truth from the dross of error in which it may be imbedded, to eliminate it from the specious fallacies with which it may be surrounded; accurately and logically to trace effects, however remote and apparently unconnected, to their causes; skillfully to combine, compare and analyze with strict reference to first principles and undeniable premises? Or do they content themselves with the authoritative communication of results satisfactorily deduced by others, the most complete mastery of which, while it may confer a show of erudition, strengthens only the memory, and substitutes a superficial gloss of learning for the real power of true science? And finally, do they conduct those committed to their charge, by a wise gradation, through the fundamental principles and varied applications of the exact sciences, over the broad and inviting fields of natural history and philosophy, to the more elevated and nobler domains of genius, imagination, poetry, art, metaphysical research and deep theological lore—regions where all the higher faculties of the human mind may "bathe in floods of living light," and plume their energies and strengthen their pinions in those "green pastures," and by the side of those "still waters," which, like Siloa's gentle stream, "flow fast by the oracles of God?"

Grievously do they err, sadly and lamentably do they misconceive the objects and purposes of that "generous culture" which constitutes all true education, who would exclude from its proper scope those "thoughts that breathe, and words that burn," which were conceived and spoken in musical accents by "the world's gray fathers" of Greece and Rome, of Palestine and Persia and Egypt, in the first faint dawn of civilization, and in the bracing, invigorating mountain air of its morning fragrance and beauty. Inexcusably, unjustifiably do they "cramp, cabin and confine" the divine faculties of the human mind, who would deprive it of ample and free communion with those master-spirits of the deathless life and song, who in all ages have cast the radiant glories of their rapt imaginations

> "Above the smoke and stir of this dim spot
> Which men call earth, and with low-thoughted care,
> Strive to keep up a frail and feverish being."

Let it not be said that these excursions into the purer and rarer atmosphere of genius and fancy

—these flights "far in the unapparent"—unfit us for the practical duties and stern requirements of this "working-day world." As well may you proscribe "Nature's sweet restorer, balmy sleep" for its thick-coming fancies, its wondrous revelations of beauty, its evanescent glimpses of the soul's transcendent greatness, "unclogged with baser matter," its vast absorption of that mere pittance, at best, of time afforded us for the great task of existence. Both our sleeping and waking fancies invigorate, strengthen and renew the mind, lift it from the stifling vapors of flesh and sense, replenish it with the pure elements of its native atmosphere, and send it down to its appointed pilgrimage of earthly struggle and suffering refreshed and reanimated for the stern battle of life. "They also serve, who only stand and wait."

"From the mount
Of high transfiguration, we come down
Into our common life-time, as the diver
Breathes upper air, a moment, e'er he plunges,
And by mere virtue of that moment, lives
In breathless caverns deep and dark."

And who that has ranged over the wilderness of sweets, the wide, extended plains of knowledge, the lofty summits of profoundest wisdom which the literature of ancient and modern times spreads out to view — who that has lingered over the classic pages of Homer and Virgil, of Plato and Cicero, of Tasso and Dante, and bathed his soul in the rich poetry and vigorous prose of Shakespeare and Milton and Spenser, of Cowper and Wordsworth, of Bryant and Longfellow and Irving, and all that immortal brotherhood of genius, whose greatness "posterity will not willingly let die" — who that has stood before the deathless creations of those heavenly-minded artists of the olden time, who have clothed the temples and palaces of Greece and the vaulted cathedrals and storied ruins of Italy with a glory and a power which modern genius has vainly essayed to rival, has not felt in the utmost recesses of his being that a "thing of beauty is," indeed, "a joy forever." Who that has listened to those immortal strains of melody and harmony, those bursts of glorified sound which, under the hands or animated by the spirits of the great composers of ancient and modern times, fill air, earth and heaven with the prolonged echoes of their lofty and spirit-stirring cadences, is not more deeply conscious of his heavenly origin, of the unspeakable greatness, the awful sanctity, the tremendous responsibilities of his mysterious being? Are we, then, justifiable in dismissing the youth of our land from our halls of learning with these immense capacities of refined enjoyments, these noble channels of the soul's activity, these abiding testimonials of its innate grandeur undeveloped and uncultivated?

The times in which we live, too, and the spirit of the age in which our lots have been cast, are fertile in great events—great discoveries in science and the arts, great revolutions of opinions and principles, great movements of the popular mind in every direction, great premonitions of the possible future. Grave questions of political and social economy, involving results of immense magnitude and importance, are agitating the deepest and profoundest intellects of our community; principles which underlie the very foundations of government and society are discussed in every quarter; vast physical changes are taking place over the surface of great continents, involving the destinies and the welfare of unborn nations, and elements are at work which in their development may and must give a new aspect to the entire civilization of the world. Are our institutions of learning of every grade taking heed of these tidal movements of the great heart of humanity, preparing their pupils for active, intelligent and earnest participation in the ebbings and flowings of that mighty current which is thus precipitating its waters over the surface of society? Are they sending out pupils fitted at all points to grapple with the gigantic enterprises of the age, to direct its energies, to impress upon it the stamp of greatness and power, to elevate and dignify its aspirations, and to restrain its excesses?

These are, in my judgment, serious and practical questions, entering, as I conceive, into the very essence of Education, involving that which alone should constitute its distinctive end and aim, the formation of character, the establishment of principles, the cultivation of every rational faculty of our being, and the right direction of the conduct and the life. In so far as our own systems of instruction, public or private, fail in the accomplishment of these high purposes—in so far as they leave a single intelligent human being destitute of that culture which his nature and the requirements of society demand—in so far as they bestow a merely superficial or imperfect development of the intellectual, moral and religious faculties, or fail to confer upon each the power of indefinite self-improvement in whatsoever direction the exigencies of life or its own enlightened impulses may prompt—in so far as they neglect to lay open before the ingenuous minds of those committed to their charge the ample treasures of ancient and modern literature, science and art in every department where the ethereal footsteps of genius and talent have passed—and in so far as they fall behind the awakened spirit of the age, and shut their eyes and ears against its visible and audible manifestations of power—to this extent they will have failed to realize the full import and to meet the full responsibilities of the high mission with which they have been charged.

I have thus, with great frankness and plainness, indicated some of those shortcomings and defects which have appeared to me to pervade our systems of public instruction and popular education. I trust that in my cursory and desultory treatment of this important topic I have not been actuated by a captious or a cynical spirit of fault-finding and censure. To me this great interest of universal education is sacred and very dear. I bless God for its wide diffusion and rapid advancement, for its numerous and varied excellencies, for the deep hold it possesses upon the public mind, for the great prospects for the future which it involves, for the glory it reflects upon our past history, and for the innumerable and inestimable benefits it has conferred upon our favored and happy land. I am deeply grateful for the opportunities which have been afforded me, for so long a period of time, to contribute to the full extent of my humble abilities to the upbuilding of its stately superstructure, and to watch over its growth and progress as it has gradually and steadily reared its proud proportions in our midst. I earnestly desire its improvement and expansion. I look not for perfection in any thing earthly, nor, were it otherwise, have I the vanity or the presumption to hope to be able to point out the direction from which its attainment might be expected. But, confiding in that indomitable spirit of progress which is the marked characteristic of the age in which we live, trusting with an abiding and unswerving faith in the might of that great IDEA which filled the souls of the Pilgrim Fathers of New England, the indissoluble connection of RELIGION and EDUCATION — the threefold cord of INTELLIGENCE, FREEDOM and CHRISTIANITY — I venture to look forward in the future to the full realization of the rich promise of the past, to the continued improvement and indefinite enlargement of that noble system on which all our hopes for the perpetuity of our free institutions rest, to the sound, complete and CHRISTIAN education of every child of the Republic. I look upon our Common

Schools, Academies, Colleges and other institutions of learning, both public and private, as the sheet-anchors of our prosperity and greatness, and, as such, I would cherish, strengthen, consolidate and improve them to their utmost possible capacity. Innumerable and unavoidable contingencies may lay waste our fertile fields, desolate our happy homes, prostrate our commerce, destroy our manufactures, paralyze our industry and dry up the springs of our enterprise, but here, in these consecrated halls and amid these quiet shades, from these Temples of learning, rearing their stately fronts in every quarter of our crowded cities, adorning and beautifying every village and hamlet of our land, and diffusing their beneficent and happy influences over every home, shall go forth those recuperative energies and that recreative power which shall again cause the "wilderness and the desolate places to bud and blossom as the rose."

"Change, wide and deep, and silently performed,
This land shall witness: and, as days roll on,
Earth's universal frame shall feel the effect,
Even till the smallest habitable rock
Beaten by lonely billows; hear the songs
Of humanized society, and bloom
With civil arts, that send their fragrance forth,
A grateful tribute to all-ruling Heaven.

From culture unexclusively bestowed
On this, our noble race, in freedom born,
Expect these mighty issues: from the pains
And faithful care of unambitious schools,
Instructing simple childhood's ready ear,
THENCE LOOK FOR THESE MAGNIFICENT RESULTS!"

CHAPTER XIV.

SCIENCE AND REVELATION—SANCTIONS AND MOTIVES —PUBLIC OPINION.

THE time has been, and that at no great distance from our own days, when the multiplied discoveries of science in the natural and physical world, and the researches and speculations of philosophers in the world of mind, were deemed alike at variance with the paramount authority of Revelation, and as at best an attempt on the part of presumptuous and misguided men to attain to the knowledge of that which transcended the limited prerogative of humanity. It seems now, however, to be conceded that true science, whether physical, intellectual or moral, can not, by any possibility, be at variance with Revelation in any of its forms. Truth is uniformly and necessarily consistent with itself. While, therefore, the imperative dictates of sound philosophy command us to reject any and every hypothesis of science, ethics or morality which contradicts the authentic testimony of Revelation, a reverential and sacred regard for truth and nature calls upon us in an equally authoritative manner to reject such an arbitrary interpretation of the latter as shall be found unwarranted by reason, observation and experience, and contradictory to the direct evidence of our unperverted senses. Interpretation only is to be subjected to this discriminating process, for an enlightened and attentive investigation and examination of the respective claims of natural and revealed knowledge will show them to be uniformly and invariably consistent and harmonious in every essential requisite. The imperishable tablets of the Christian faith can never be marred or dimmed by contact with true science, sound philosophy, and advancing civilization and knowledge. On the contrary, the law and the testimony there inscribed by the finger of Almighty Wisdom will become the more legible, luminous and clear in proportion as they are subjected to the tests of an expanded and enlightened observation—the practical deductions slowly evolved from the experience of ages—and the progressive discoveries in science and the arts. They have nothing to fear from the utmost advancement of human wisdom and improvement; and it is when the pestilential miasma of passion, guilt and crime sheds its baleful influence over the human intellect, obscuring its perceptions, blighting its energies and perverting its developments, that we are called upon to draw the line of demarkation between Religion and Science, Reason and Revelation, the God of the Bible, and the Author and Disposer of Nature.

When we look abroad upon the troubled ocean of human life and witness the constant and restless agitation of its surface, strewn with the melancholy wrecks of ages — now dashing into fragments many a noble and stately bark, freighted with the highest hopes of nations, communities and individuals, now whelming under its impetuous and undiscerning billows the nameless, humble and obscure voyager upon the trackless path — experiencing in its ceaseless commotion apparently no interval of repose and no relaxation of its mad impulses, we may well ask ourselves what power short of Omnipotence can control its excited and turbulent career, or say to its rebellious fury, "Thus far shalt thou come, but no farther; and here shall thy proud waves be stayed." There is a point beyond which philosophy can not penetrate; where reason and intellect and all the faculties of the human mind are powerless and impotent, and where nothing remains to the loftiest genius, in common with the humblest and most uninstructed range of thought, but to wonder, to adore and submit. Even the human mind, that most stupendous workmanship of Infinite Wisdom, that emanation from the Divine essence, has its laws which it can not disobey if it would, its limitations which it may not overpass. There are mysteries connected with our existence here which eternity alone can solve—relations to which flesh and blood can never penetrate—links which earthly vision can never discover—causes beyond the cognizance of mortality—and effects incapable of being fully traced by any intellectual powers conferred on mere humanity. It is idle, it is worse than idle, it is impious, to indulge the vain fancy that any conceivable advancement of the race in wisdom, any possible condition of society, or any attainable purification of the grosser elements of our nature can suffice to perfect our knowledge of the moral government of the world in which we live or initiate us into the grand scope and ultimate designs of the Creator in the multifarious and complicated labyrinths of human existence and destiny. Nor is it in any degree necessary for our happiness here, or our welfare hereafter, that the inscrutable records of the Book of Fate should be exposed to our view. It requires but a brief experience to enable us to comprehend the existence and become aware, in some small degree at least, of the influence of those elementary laws of being which circumscribe us on every hand, to learn that it is only by a general obedience to these laws that we can secure an exemption from the formidable evils which encompass us, and to be assured that by a systematic and habitual neglect, or a gross infraction of any of these laws, we incur a penalty proportioned to our departure from their requirements. It is only necessary to extend and faithfully apply the principle thus deduced from our ordinary experience, to enable us to arrive at the more important but not less obvious inference that the laws thus prescribed are uniform in their operation, invariable in their nature, unyielding and inflexible in their demands upon our obedience, and admitting of no departure from their requisitions, however inconsiderable, without exacting the penalty. But this is a conclusion by no means intuitively or without difficulty attained in practice, under the most auspicious and favorable circumstances incident to humanity. The records of history, and the process which passes within our own breasts as leaf after leaf of the volume of existence is unfolded to our perception, demonstrate that the lessons which bring with them increased wisdom, increased knowledge of the human heart, increasing happiness and progressive virtue, are slowly and painfully evolved from the shattered wrecks of the past, from the consequences of manifold and long aberration from rectitude, from incessant observation and combinations of the diversified elements of experience, and from a bitter novitiate in the stern school of adversity and suffering. Of the hundreds of millions of human beings whom each successive generation as it passes on sends "to take their places in the halls of death," how comparatively few is the number of those who have been able to solve the deep problem of their own existence and being, or to ascertain and apply the unvarying and necessary connection between the laws of nature and of its Creator, and the enjoyment of happiness! How vast the number of those who have ignorantly or presumptuously, but constantly, violated those laws, and paid the bitter penalty in wretchedness and misery, physical and mental, protracted, with occasional and evanescent intervals of comparative enjoyment, to the verge of a longer or shorter career! We are unwilling to concede, at least to the extent claimed by some severe moralists of every age, the existence of those moral and intellectual phenomena which have afforded frequent and mournful themes for the indignant reprobation of the wise and good —where the path of duty has been plainly apprehended, the guilt and the consequences of a departure from it clearly perceived, and yet that departure deliberately determined upon and persisted in with a full knowledge that happiness and peace, innocency and virtue were irrevocably renounced. We are disposed to view the melancholy obliquities of our common nature in a more favorable and charitable light, and to attribute the lamentable dereliction from its original purity, which the world has ever witnessed and which succeeding ages will probably long continue to witness, rather to ignorance of the fundamental laws of being than to a bold and enlightened but most presumptuous defiance of those laws, with a clear apprehension of the inevitable consequences. It can not be, that a reasoning, intelligent and well-balanced mind should voluntarily choose to descend from the proud eminence of virtuous innocence to the lowest depths of profligacy and vice; or that a human being, endowed with the most perfect physical organization, and painfully alive to the nicest sensibilities of its nature, should not only look with indifference upon a life of protracted suffering, opening no vista of hope and admitting of no alleviation or solace this side of eternity, but should, as the result of his unbiased will and free choice, link his destiny to such a career of ignominy and degradation—so withering, so hopeless, and so accursed by God and by man. It is believed that no one can discover, upon the most faithful examination of his own mental and moral faculties, any well-founded conception, any feeling or emotion corresponding to a principle so revolting to humanity, any law of his own being from which he can legitimately infer a result so deplorable. The Author of our being has indeed rendered such a combination morally impossible. It would be in palpable and direct opposition to all we know, or can upon rational principles conceive, of infinite benevolence and wisdom, that seeks only the highest good of all its subjects; it would present an anomaly in the moral machinery of the universe—the intermingling of elements in our common nature in irreconcilable enmity with each other, governed by contradictory laws and leading to the most opposite and discordant results. That "the heart of man is deceitful above all things, and desperately wicked;" that its every "imagination is evil, and that continually," the experience of all ages, and the solemn declarations of revelation coincide in establishing; but we may surely indulge in the supposition that the depravity and wickedness which has uniformly characterized mankind has not been of that deep dye which fully comprehended and deliberately rejected its own highest happiness, which clearly discerned the inevitable retributions of disobedience, and yet "rushed upon the thick bosses of the buckler" of the avenger.

We are aware that this is in some measure debatable ground; but we are also aware that its boundaries have not been so strictly defined as to preclude us from the effort to reclaim millions of wanderers from the heavy imputation of apostasy from the pale of humanity. While we can not but lament the deplorable infatuation which has deprived the great mass of our fellowmen in every age of the natural heritage of happiness bestowed upon them at their birth, and condemned them to misery and remorse and the complicated ills of a degenerate world, we may at least be permitted to indulge the consoling reflection that this severe and calamitous portion was not the necessary result of a nature altogether perverted from its original purity, and wholly incapable of producing less bitter fruits. "The

Eden of human nature," says an eloquent writer of our own day, "has, indeed, long been trampled down and desolated, and storms waste it continually; nevertheless the soil is still rich with the germ of its pristine beauty, the colors of Paradise are sleeping in the clods, and a little favor, a little protection and a little culture shall show what once was there." A beautiful and ennobling sentiment, and well worthy of all acceptation. Much of the harsh censoriousness with which human frailty, ignorance and delusion has at all times been visited by those whom a more fortunate and enviable mental organization has exempted from temptation or crime might well have been spared, had this elevated and catholic spirit of Christian benevolence prevailed more generally. In our investigations into the motives, conduct and character of our fellow-men, it is much wiser and far less dangerous to err on the side of charity and mercy than their opposites; and certainly, if it be our aim to advance the standard of intellectual and moral improvement, and to elevate the condition of our species, it is equally unphilosophical and unjust to assume in the outset that the task is hopeless and impracticable.

The conclusion to which these observations

tend is obvious. Man is susceptible, in his own proper nature, of the highest intelligence, virtue and consequent happiness which was originally bestowed upon humanity by creative wisdom and benevolence; but by reason of his peculiar mental and moral organization, adapted to progressive advancement but left free to work out its own destiny, and in consequence of the powerful and constantly accumulating influences which surround him from infancy, he contracts insensibly, and at a very early period, the tendency to go astray from that very narrow and restricted path of duty. The impulse which hurries him on from one successive step to another of error, guilt and retribution, is seldom if ever the result of his own deliberate choice and enlightened knowledge of the laws of being, and the consequences of their infringement. He is impelled by the operation of strong and unchecked passions, the consequences of a neglected or perverted education in some of its numerous forms; and, through ignorance in a great measure of his own nature, capacities and destination, inability to withstand temptation, and the presence and influence of a great variety of powerful external and internal impulses, the voice of reason, judgment, and often of conscience, is gradually and imperceptibly stifled; the intellectual functions transmit erroneous information; the moral faculties lose their ascendancy, and the empire of the mind degenerates into hopeless anarchy and inextricable confusion.

From this view of the subject the immense importance of an enlightened and extended system of physical, intellectual and moral education is obvious; one by which, at the earliest period when such knowledge can be comprehended, we may be accurately informed of the peculiar constitution of our nature, its powers and faculties, their modes of manifestation and their various operation, whether in accordance with their own innate force or influenced by the external world of matter or of mind.

Upon this broad and comprehensive foundation a superstructure may be reared of solid and durable materials, fitted to resist the incessant elemental warfare of the passions, and providing an impregnable rampart against every hostile attack. If it be true that the great mass of crime and wretchedness, of suffering and of woe, with which the world is filled may be traced directly or remotely to ignorance; if it be also true that all the happiness and enjoyment of which humanity is susceptible proceed from and are the invariable and necessary result of an adherence to the laws impressed by the Creator upon all the workmanship of his hands; and if, moreover, such an adherence is entirely practicable and attainable and becomes instantly its own reward, considerations of the most solemn and momentous import, as well to ourselves as to the race to which we belong, and involving the welfare of the present and future generations, impel us to begin the great work of an education which shall be commensurate with our high nature and destiny, and which shall enable us so to live as to secure the utmost happiness of which our being is capable.

It may with safety be admitted that a well-regulated and well-directed public opinion is a more efficient agent in the work of education than all the systems of instruction which have been or can be devised in its absence. If the prevailing tendency of the age and of the community in which we live be favorable to a progressive advancement in wisdom and virtue and knowledge—as the basis of the only sound philosophy of human life, as worthy of a general concentration of all its interests, passions and feelings—the mind and the heart will insensibly and involuntarily take that direction, the moral powers will assume their proper preponderance, and all the various faculties of our nature will harmoniously co-operate in their respective spheres. If, on the other hand, the attainment of wealth, the pursuit of pleasure, the struggle for power, for distinction and for worldly applause are found to be the principal objects of ambition, and to engross the energies of the mass of mankind, the most perfect system of education will fail in accomplishing any permanent results, or in securing any general adoption.

It is but too true that the great obstacle to the successful prosecution of the most thoroughly digested and well-considered system of popular education is found in the powerful influence of a perverted public opinion operating with an irresistible force upon the most striking tendencies and pursuits of life. It is in vain to impress upon the mind, amid the congenial associations of youth, innocence and happiness, the purest doctrines of the most elevated philosophy, if, when the hallowed sanctuary of home is overpassed, and the delightful groves of the academy left behind, the sober realities of life are discovered to be a compound of interested selfishness, unworthy aspirations and unchastened ambition, while nobler views, nobler efforts and a more exalted benevolence seldom find a congenial atmosphere where they may bud, blossom and expand. It is in vain to expatiate upon the beauty and the sublimity of moral excellence, while the world's ready and unbounded applause awaits the successful results of bold effrontery, low duplicity, persevering cunning and well-dissembled craft. The highest order of intellect, combined with the sternest moral and religious principles, can rarely mingle with the baser elements of the busy world and escape the deep contamination of the contact.

There are few circumstances and conditions in life in which we can render ourselves to any extent independent of the powerful influence which the opinions of those around us and the public at large exert upon our conduct. There is a principle deeply implanted in our nature which compels us uniformly to regulate even our most trivial actions, and gradually to form our character and mould our sentiments, by the standard which prevails in the community to which we belong. History affords ample evidence of the presence and the effects of this all-pervading power, and hence the formidable obstacles which have in all ages been interposed to the progress of those great reforms in religion, moral and political economy and science, which from time to time have agitated society to its centre. The minds and actions of men so insensibly assimilate to each other, and so imperceptibly is the power of public opinion concentrated around the established institutions, modes of thinking and ordinary pursuits of the day, that the slightest innovation upon the magic circle drawn by habit, by custom and by association, excites at once the astonishment and indignation of all, and places the daring offender beyond the pale of pardon.

It is needless tò adduce instances abounding in the annals of our race of the melancholy effects of this potent influence. All of the elevation to which the morals, the intellect and the refinement of the present age has attained, has been imparted to it by the slow and painful development of principles promulgated in the face of danger and often of death, and maintained in the midst of a fiery struggle against principalities and powers and a world in arms, madly bent upon the overthrow of champions of whom indeed it was not worthy. We are accustomed to flatter ourselves, in these days of greater enlightenment and wisdom, that a more correct appreciation of the great truths of the moral and physical world places us at an immeasurable distance from the erroneous influences of those ages of darkness and gloom. Thanks to the expanding spirit of a progressive civilization, this proud boast is to a great extent borne out by the evidence of facts. Under the peculiar and inestimable institutions of our own favored land, the intellect and the heart are, indeed, left free to accomplish their highest conceptions without the most remote apprehension of physical restraint. But these institutions, while they have wisely interposed the most efficient checks to the introduction of a persecuting and an intolerant spirit, have, at the same time, conferred an overwhelming power upon the influence of public opinion. Before that power the highest and the lowest are compelled, by a moral force which it is in vain to withstand, to bow with an implicit deference. To this mighty power let us then appeal for another and a powerful sanction to our great system of Universal Education, and, with the continued favor and blessing of Divine Providence, let us trustfully hope for the diffusion of knowledge wherever a human being exists to participate in its benefits!

CHAPTER XV.

OBJECTS, MEANS AND ENDS OF EDUCATION.

IN all our efforts to improve and perfect our systems of Public Instruction, it is of paramount importance clearly to understand and constantly to keep in view the objects, aims and ends of Education. These are manifold and various—comprehending not only the happiness and well-being of individuals, but of communities, states and nations—not only the interests of the present but of the future—not only the destinies of time, but of eternity.

Education is the formation of character, in all its aspects, in all the possibilities of its development and expansion here and hereafter. It is the cultivation, training and discipline of every faculty of the intellect, and every affection and disposition of the moral and religious nature, for the attainment and the fulfillment of the great purposes for which existence was conferred.

That culture which regards exclusively or primarily the mere attainment of knowledge, to whatsoever extent it may be carried, or to whatsoever degree of advancement it may be enabled to arrive, can not be otherwise than essentially and fatally defective. And yet it is not to be denied that hitherto the course of instruction in all our systems of Popular Education, public and private, has far too generally assumed this direction. Hence, while the boundaries of science have been almost indefinitely extended in every direction, and while knowledge has been almost universally diffused throughout every civilized community, no corresponding advancement has been made in public and private morality and virtue. On the other hand, we are assured, upon the most unquestionable authority, and there is unfortunately but little room to doubt the fact, that the increase of vice and crime, and the prevalence of dishonesty and of open and secret fraud and corruption, have been more than proportionate to the increase of population and the advancement of our modern civilization. In a community like our own, where the great mass of the population have enjoyed the advantage of early and continued education during the period ordinarily allotted to instruction — where, too, such instruction is entirely free to all, and nearly universal in fact—where the various sciences and the arts, especially those which have any relation to the pursuits and wants of practical life, have been carried to the highest attainable excellence, it might reasonably be expected that the criminal calendar, instead of annually increasing, should rapidly and steadily be diminished—that a high standard, both of public and private morality, should prevail, and that the upright, the virtuous and the good should be effectually secured against the depredations of the vicious, and the burden of their maintenance and support. If this result has not been attained, or is not likely to be attained—if the generous and ample expenditures which have been and continue to be lavished upon the education of the youth of our land, produce no perceptible amelioration in the tone of public or private morals, and diminish in no perceptible ratio the expenses of repressing and punishing crime, or of supporting the worthless and the dissolute—the inference would seem to be a legitimate one, either that the influence of education for the improvement and elevation of humanity has been overrated, or that it has hitherto failed, in a most important and essential respect, in availing itself of the proper means for the accomplishment of its object. Such a conclusion, however, would be premature and fallacious, unwarranted by the real facts of the case, and unsupported by any substantial foundation in sound reasoning or argument from those facts.

The importance of a general and universal diffusion of useful knowledge among the citizens of a free state has not been and can not be overrated. Its necessary and inevitable tendency is, and must be, under all and any circumstances, to augment, in a steadily increasing ratio, all those elements of individual and social prosperity and advancement which in the aggregate constitute national greatness. Nor is it, to any considerable extent or degree, from the educated portion of the population of any country that the ranks of vice, crime and mendicity are recruited. Seldom, indeed, is the public mind startled with the annunciation of the arrest, trial and conviction of an intelligent and well-educated criminal; and still more rare is it to find such an individual dependent upon public charity for maintenance and support. The most scrutinizing and careful examination of the records of our criminal courts, prisons, penitentiaries and almshouses will be found to establish the fact that at least ninety out of every hundred on their calendars, and probably a much larger proportion of the whole number for any given series of years, have never, or but very imperfectly, availed themselves of the facilities for education which are afforded by our common schools, defective and incomplete in many respects as have been and still are these elementary institutions of learning. Not one in two hundred of these convicts, nor one in two thousand of the inmates of our almshouses, can make the slightest pretensions to what may be termed a good education, or a complete and thorough course of instruction. While, therefore, it may be true that the progress of crime and pauperism has increased in a fearful and alarming ratio to the increase of population and the progress of civilization among us, it is also clearly demonstrable that this increase is due almost exclusively to the failure to bring within the pale of our educational systems that large class of our population who stand most in need of its elevating and reforming influences. It is not because education, in the true sense of the term, is universally diffused, but because, practically and in point of fact, it is *not;* because thousands and tens of thousands of those for whose intellectual and moral culture abundant facilities have been provided have refused or omitted to avail themselves of those facilities.

Still, it is not to be denied that our institutions of instruction, public and private, our Common Schools, Academies, Colleges and Universities, are not doing what they might and should for the education of those committed to their charge. Much, very much, has indeed been accomplished through their agency in extending the boundaries of useful and practical knowledge, and instilling into the minds of the youth of our land those principles and imbuing them with those habits which, rightly improved and steadily adhered to, will seldom fail to guard them effectually against the numerous snares and pitfalls which await them on every hand in the journey of life. That they have not done more —that education itself has not assumed the form and occupied the position of the first and highest of the sciences, and the noblest and most important of the arts—that it has not been made to comprehend not only the entire circle of practical and attainable knowledge, but to confer in all its amplitude and to its fullest extent the power of self-culture, self-control, and self-advancement—that it has not taken cognizance of all the various faculties of our being, and given full and complete and harmonious development to each in accordance with the great purposes of existence here and hereafter — that these principles and views have not more generally been recognized and acted upon, may readily be accounted for, though not fully justified, when we consider the numerous disadvantages and obstacles with which even our best institutions of learning are forced to contend. The want of an adequate and independent support, of an intimate connection and relation with other similar institutions and with those of a different grade—the too rigid and inflexible adherence to modes of instruction and systems of intellectual and moral discipline which the advancement of science and the progress of modern civilization have rendered inapplicable to the existing state of things; these, combined with the restless and uncontrollable desire of the ardent and ambitious student to plunge at the earliest possible period into the pursuits and to grasp the prizes of active life, have exerted a powerful influence in restricting and circumscribing the legitimate domain of education.

Without entering at this time upon the discussion of the question whether a public or private education is most conducive to the future welfare of the pupil, it is unquestionably both the interest and the duty of every community to provide at the public expense every possible facility for the complete and thorough education of the young, and to take the most effectual measures to bring within the scope of the means thus furnished every child not otherwise suitably provided for in this respect. Both the public welfare and the safety and security of individuals imperatively demand that none of the members of the community should be permitted to grow up in ignorance, with its almost invariable attendants, vice, destitution and crime. It is not enough that the doors of our noble and liberally distributed temples of knowledge are thrown freely and invitingly open to every child—it is not enough that the amplest and most lavish means are annually appropriated for the extension and diffusion of our system of public instruction—while at the same time we are compelled to contribute still more liberally to the repression, the detection and punishment of crime, and the support of vagabondism and mendicity. We have it in our power to *prevent* these evils, to a very great extent, by cutting off their source—by requiring, at the hands of parents, guardians or employers of youth, that the children confided to their care shall, in some way, be properly and adequately instructed, and at all events that they shall not, under any pretense, be allowed to remain in utter and hopeless ignorance, exposed to the nefarious designs of the profligate and unprincipled, and the numerous temptations incident to poverty and want. The community has the right, and it is its duty to require that the liberal and munificent outlay which it invests in the education of its citizens shall not be virtually counteracted, or rendered unavailing to the accomplishment of the purposes for which it is designed, by the culpable and criminal neglect of a large portion of its members to avail themselves of the facilities thus placed at their disposal. It has a right, and it is its duty, to insist that for every dollar contributed toward the education of the people, at least an equal amount shall be deducted from the annual assessment for the maintenance and punishment of criminals and the support of vagabonds and paupers; and this result it can secure only by gathering into the institutions of learning provided for that purpose *all* those of a suitable age for whose mental and moral culture no other adequate provision has been made.

This course is not only dictated by considerations of interest and of policy, so far as the public are concerned, but it commends itself to our adoption as eminently in accordance with the principles of an enlightened Christian philanthropy. The full extent of the wretchedness, destitution, ignorance and crime which has been permitted to accumulate in our great metropolis from this single source can not, of course, in the absence of the requisite statistical details, be accurately stated; but from information derived from the most reliable sources, there can exist no reasonable doubt that at the very least thirty thousand children are utterly unprovided with the means of education, and surrounded by influences most unfavorable to honesty and morality. Many thousands of these children are virtually homeless, houseless, suffering and wretched outcasts of humanity—unacquainted with the rudiments of knowledge—associating only with the vile, the unprincipled and the vicious—familiar only with misery, violence, cruelty, hunger and pain—and taught and forced to regard all around them as their natural enemies, of whom every possible advantage is to be taken. They wage an incessant war upon the community, and by their numbers, their precocity in vice, their pressing necessities and the utter recklessness of their characters, speedily render themselves formidable recruits in the ranks of crime. After a longer or shorter career of successful depredation, they become the inmates of our prisons, penitentiaries and almshouses, and drag out a miserable and infamous existence, unenlightened by a single spark of intellect and unaccompanied by a solitary gleam of Christian virtue or rational happiness. How different would be the result if these neglected children of vice and destitution were earnestly, systematically and diligently sought out, taken by the hand, their wants supplied, their education, intellectual and moral, cared for, and their associations with infamy and degradation cut off at their source! And how worthy of a Christian community like our own, through its appropriate municipal organs, and at the common charge of all its members, thus to gather within the fold of its comprehensive benevolence these miserable waifs and strays of humanity—thus effectually and permanently to reclaim them from the very depths of ignorance and wretchedness, train them to habits of usefulness, imbue them with principles of goodness and virtue, and confer upon them all the requisite means and instrumentalities of future well-being, honor and happiness! There on the one hand are the thousands and tens of thousands of ignorant, suffering, degraded, vicious and homeless children—destined, inevitably, in a few years to become the active scourges, the irreclaimable pests, and the heavy burden of the community; and here, on the other, are our stately, noble, commodious and comfortable Free Public Schools, provided, prepared and furnished at the public expense, open and ready for the reception of all, of every grade and every rank. Why not, then, in the true spirit of an active and enlightened Christian beneficence, "go out into the highways and hedges," the by-ways and purlieus, the lowest haunts of poverty and infamy and vice, and, if necessary, "compel them to come in"—not by force, not by pains and penalties, but by the stronger cords of persevering, systematic, well-directed kindness and sympathy, put forth not alone by individuals and associations and charitable organizations, but by the entire community in its corporate capacity for its own benefit equally with theirs?

The liberal and generous policy of the State, therefore, in establishing and munificently supporting schools in every locality, however restricted or obscure, where children are to be found to avail themselves of their advantages, and in opening these schools freely and without charge to all who may desire to attend upon their instructions, has abundantly vindicated itself by the practical results which have followed its adoption, even though it may not have accomplished all which its advocates expected or desired, or secured all the advantages of which it is fairly susceptible. It has conferred the priceless blessings of education to a greater or less extent upon millions of those who are now or are hereafter to become citizens of the Republic; and among those who have enjoyed and faithfully improved these blessings, ninety-nine out of every hundred have been and promise to become useful, intelligent and upright members of society—the guardians and supporters of morality and order, the advancers of civilization and the dispensers of knowledge and virtue. That ignorance and immorality, vice and crime, destitution and misery still so extensively prevail, keeping pace with the advancement of our population and the progress of knowledge, and that education does not fully realize all the beneficial results which may reasonably be expected from its general diffusion, may, it is believed, satisfactorily be accounted for—

First.—By the fact that there are still permitted to remain and to grow up to maturity in our midst a vast number of children and youth wholly destitute of instruction or of moral and religious culture, and that the character, condition and influence of this portion of our population are necessarily productive of the most disastrous and injurious results — rendering comparatively inefficacious, so far at least as the public burdens are concerned, the immense outlay annually expended for the entire education of the youth of the State.

Second.—By the fact that a large proportion of those who are brought to some extent within the influences of our public and private schools are not permitted to avail themselves of their course of instruction and mental and moral discipline for a sufficient length of time to enable them to derive any permanent and substantial advantage.

Third.—By the fact that in a large class of cases the education and discipline of these institutions, however excellent and valuable they may be in themselves, are counteracted and neutralized by opposing influences at home and amid the scenes and associations of every-day life; and,

Fourth.—By the fact that this education and discipline, even under the most favorable auspices, and when it embraces the whole period of youth, is frequently and to a great extent defective—

1. In not being sufficiently *comprehensive*, failing to embrace in its culture the whole nature of the child, physical, intellectual, moral and religious, and omitting or neglecting that assiduous, careful and conscientious training and discipline of the affections and passions upon which so essential a part of the future character is destined inevitably to depend.

2. In not being sufficiently *practical*, expending a disproportionate share of its energies in the accomplishment of results, which, however valuable they may be in a purely scientific point of view, or however useful and even indispensable under special and peculiar circumstances, are of little practical value in the ordinary pursuits of life, and under the actual circumstances and condition and with reference to the probable future wants of the pupil.

3. In not providing adequate means and facilities for the complete preparation and training of teachers of the highest grade of character and

qualifications, and in failing to offer sufficient pecuniary inducements to secure permanently the services of such a class of teachers.

What are the great paramount evils with which society and communities have ever been and still are obliged to contend, rendering property and persons alike insecure, and compelling the continued maintenance, at an enormous cost, of civil and criminal tribunals for the administration and enforcement of justice, the support of paupers, and the punishment and repression of crime? Are they not, primarily and chiefly, ignorance, and its almost inseparable concomitants, poverty, wretchedness and vice? Who can entertain a reasonable doubt that if every child, whatever may be the circumstances or condition of his parent, could be placed at the age of four or five years under the charge of fully qualified and competent teachers, in institutions specially provided for that purpose by the authority of the State, and subjected for a period of ten or twelve years to a wise, judicious and enlightened culture and discipline of all the physical, intellectual, moral and religious faculties of his nature, side by side with all the other children of the community, pauperism and immorality and vice and crime, in all their innumerable manifestations, would entirely disappear, or be restricted within such narrow limits that they would no longer disturb the peace, or prey as they now do upon the vitals of society? Two conditions only are requisite for the full accomplishment of this most desirable object: the first, that the process of education and instruction should be thorough and complete, embracing in their fullest extent all the faculties of our being, and harmoniously developing and judiciously directing all the varied powers of our common nature; and, secondly, that this education and instruction should not only be freely offered to every child, but that efficient measures should be adopted to ensure its reception, either in institutions provided by the State, or in such other mode as parents should prefer. If our public schools are not sufficiently numerous or spacious to afford the requisite accommodations for this purpose, let them at whatever cost be increased, extended and enlarged. If the requisite supply of faithful, competent, skillful and successful teachers falls short of the demand, let adequate pecuniary and personal inducements be presented until the deficiency be fully met. If false and imperfect ideas of education prevail, if the standard of instruction and of moral and intellectual discipline prove inadequate in any of its departments to the accomplishment of the object in view—the formation and development of a noble, manly, generous and exalted character—let the highest energies of the first minds of the community be brought to bear upon its improvement and perfection.

The most accurate and reliable statistics, carefully gathered from the official records of our own and other countries, conclusively show that, imperfect and defective as our systems of education are and have been—too generally confined in their widest scope to the mere communication of intellectual instruction, and even that frequently in the crudest form and during only a very brief and intermitted period of time—they have, nevertheless, served to draw a clear, distinct and sharply-defined line between pauperism and crime on the one hand, and uprightness, intelligence, usefulness and an independent competency on the other. With very rare exceptions the inmates of our almshouses and pauper asylums—institutions for the support of which we contribute annually a sum nearly equal to the entire expenses of our educational system—are destitute of even an ordinary common school education, by far the greater portion of them being unable to read or write. This immense and burdensome drain upon the resources of the community might, it is clear, be dried up at its fountain by an enlightened system of general education, brought home to the doors of every child of penury and destitution. More than half of the inmates of our prisons and penitentiaries of every grade are almost entirely destitute of the simplest rudiments of education; and of the residue but a very inconsiderable proportion have enjoyed the benefits of even the lowest common school instruction. The closest and most searching analysis of the records of crime in our own city and state for the past twenty years will disclose the names of but very few individuals who have in early youth enjoyed the advantages of what, in accordance with the highest standard prevailing at the time, may be denominated a good education. Of 1122 persons, being the whole number reported by the sheriffs of the different counties of this state as under conviction and punishment for crime during the year 1847, 22 had received a "common education;" 10 only, a "tolerably good education," and 6 only were reported as "well educated." Of 1345 criminals so returned for the year 1848, 23 only had a common, 13 a tolerably good, and 10 only a good education. The whole number of persons returned to the office of the Secretary of

State as having been convicted of crime in the several counties and cities of the state during a period of nine consecutive years, from 1840 to 1848 both inclusive, was 27,949; of these 1182 were returned as having received a "common education," 414 as having a "tolerably good education," and 128 only as "well-educated." Of the remaining 26,225, only about one-half were able to read and write. The residue were destitute of any education whatever. Of the 566 boys in the House of Refuge for juvenile delinquents in this city, 287 had attended school less than six months, and 41 only had attended any public school in the city over three years. An examination of the Auburn State Prison, made a few years since, gave out of 244 prisoners but 39 who could either read or write, and but 59 who could read well. In the Connecticut State Prison, but about one-half of the convicts, when committed, knew how to write. In the Philadelphia Penitentiary, out of 217 prisoners received on its organization in 1835, 85 only could read or write, and most of these could do so only in a very imperfect manner. In the criminal statistics of France and England it has been customary to divide the convicts into four distinct classes as it respects their degree of education and instruction. 1st, those unable to read and write; 2d, those able to read and write imperfectly; 3d, those able to read and write well; 4th, those superiorly instructed. In the former country, during a period of seven consecutive years, the proportion of those embraced in the fourth class as "superiorly educated" was 227 to 9773 in the three former classes. In Scotland, where the proportional number of well-educated persons is much greater than in France, the proportion in 1836 of the fourth class to the other three was 188 to 9812, while in England it was only 91 to 9909. The whole number convicted of crime in a single year in England and Wales was 20,984, of whom 7033 were unable to read and write, 10,983 could read and write imperfectly, 2215 could read and write well, while only 191 were superiorly instructed. In Scotland, out of 2922 convicts during the same period, but 55 were enumerated in the latter class, and 2539 in the three former. In the city of Manchester, England, the police returns for the first six months of the year 1842 show that 8341 persons were taken into custody, of whom 4617 could neither read nor write, and similar statistics are to be found in the police returns of Birmingham and Leeds for the same year. The proportion of the wholly uneducated adults in the various pauper establishments of England and America is substantially the same as those above enumerated in reference to convictions for crime.

So much for the actual relations which incontrovertible facts, on both sides of the Atlantic, have demonstrated to exist between education, even in its lowest and most imperfect forms, and the annals of crime. These facts establish, on the most competent testimony, the conclusion that considerably over one-half of the inmates of our prisons and penitentiaries are destitute even of the simplest rudiments of common school instruction, and that of the remaining half a very small proportion only have enjoyed the full advantages of such a system of education as has hitherto prevailed. They show, positively and clearly, that the ranks of crime and vice are almost exclusively recruited from the ignorant classes of the community; and that precisely in proportion as knowledge is disseminated and education advanced, vice and crime recede. It must be borne in mind, in weighing these results, that the highest standard of education prevailing during the period to which they refer was far inferior, both in quantity and quality, to that which is now universally diffused among us, and that we are far—very far—from even attainable perfection in this respect. Let us now see what, upon equally competent and reliable testimony, we may reasonably hope and expect to accomplish by a faithful improvement of the best means of education we actually possess.

Several years since, a circular letter was addressed by the Hon. Horace Mann, then Secretary of the Massachusetts Board of Education, to the most distinguished and experienced educators in different sections of the Union, with the view of ascertaining their opinions, based upon long and careful observation and practical results, on "the efficiency, in the formation of social and moral character, of a good common school education, conducted on the cardinal principles of the New England system; in other words, how much of improvement, in the upright conduct and good morals of the community, might be reasonably hoped and expected if all our common schools were what they should be, what some of them now are, and what all of them, by means which the public is perfectly able to command, may soon be made to become." The specific inquiry, the answer to which constituted the object of the circular, was then clearly and distinctly presented: "Under the soundest and most vigorous system of education which we now can command, what proportion or percentage of all the children who are born can be made useful and exemplary men, honest dealers, conscientious jurors, true witnesses, incorruptible voters or magistrates, good parents, good neighbors, good members of society? In other words, with our present knowledge of the art and science of education, and with such new fruit of experience as time may be expected to bear — what proportion or percentage of all the children must be pronounced irreclaimable and irredeemable, notwithstanding the most vigorous educational efforts which in the present state of society can be put forth in their behalf? What proportion or percentage must become drunkards, profane swearers, detractors, vagabonds, rioters, cheats, thieves, aggressors upon the rights of property, of person, of reputation, or of life; or, in a single phrase, must be guilty of such omissions of right and commission of wrong, that it would have been better for the community had they never been born?" "Should all of our schools be kept by teachers of high intellectual and moral qualifications, and should all the children in the community be brought within these schools for ten months in a year, from the age of four to that of sixteen years;

then what proportion, what percentage, of such children as you have under your care could, in your opinion, be so educated and trained that their existence, on going out into the world, would be a benefit and not a detriment, an honor and not a shame, to society?"

To this circular, replies were promptly received from the distinguished educators to whom it was addressed, without consultation with each other, which, regarded as the deliberate conclusions and earnest convictions of the highest minds engaged in the educational field of labor of the Union, are entitled to the fullest confidence and regard. After an experience of more than forty years as an instructor of youth of both sexes and all ages, the venerable Dr. John Griscom of New Jersey says: "My belief is, that under the conditions mentioned in the question, not more than two per cent. of the first generation submitted to the experiment would be irreclaimable nuisances to society, and that *ninety-five* per cent. would be supporters of the moral welfare of the community." David P. Page, then Principal of the New York State Normal School, after an experience of twenty years as an educator of the highest rank, says: "Could I be connected with a school furnished with all the appliances you name, where all the children should be in constant attendance upon my instruction for a succession of years, where all my fellow-teachers should be such as you suppose, and where all the favorable influences described in your circular should surround me and cheer me, even with my moderate abilities as a teacher, I should scarcely expect, after the first generation of children submitted to the experiment, to fail *in a single case* to secure the result you have named. I should not forgive myself, nor think myself longer fit to be a teacher, if, with all the aids and influences you have supposed, I should fail in one case in a hundred to rear up children who, when they should become men, would be 'honest dealers, conscientious jurors, true witnesses, incorruptible voters or magistrates, good parents, good neighbors, good members of society,' or, as you express it in another place, who would be 'temperate, industrious, frugal, conscientious in all their dealings, prompt to pity and instruct ignorance, instead of ridiculing it and taking advantage of it, public-spirited, philanthropic, and observers of all things sacred.'" Solomon Adams, Esq., of Boston, after an experience of twenty-four years as a teacher, says: "So far as my own experience goes, so far as my knowledge of the experience of others extends, so far as the statistics of crime throw any light on the subject, I should confidently expect that *ninety-nine in a hundred*, and I think *even more*, with such means of education as you have supposed, and with such divine favor as we are authorized to expect, would become good members of society, the supporters of order, and law, and truth, and justice, and all righteousness." The Rev. Jacob Abbott of New York, an experienced and accomplished educator, says: "If all our schools were under the charge of teachers possessing what I regard as the right intellectual and moral qualifications, and if all the children of the community were brought under the influence of these schools for ten months in the year, I think that the work of training up *the whole community* to intelligence and virtue would soon be accomplished as completely as any human end could be obtained by human means." F. A. Adams, Esq., of New Jersey, says: "In the course of my experience, for ten years, in teaching between three hundred and four hundred children—mostly boys—I have been acquainted with *not more than two pupils* in regard to whom I should not feel a cheerful and strong confidence in the success of the proposed experiment." E. A. Andrews, Esq., of New Britain, Connecticut, after a connection of more than fifty years with the public and private schools of that State as pupil and teacher, and an experience of more than twenty years in the latter capacity, says: "If, *as I fully believe*, it is in the power of the people in any state, by means so simple as your question supposes, and so completely in their own power as these obviously are, so to change the whole face of society in a single generation, that *scarcely one or two per cent.* of really incorrigible members shall be found, it can not be that so great a good will continue to be neglected, and the means of its attainment unemployed." Roger S. Howard, Esq., of Vermont, after fifteen years' experience as a teacher in Newburyport, Massachusetts, bears the following direct and explicit testimony to the value and efficacy of a good common-school system: "Judging from what I have seen and do know, if the conditions you have mentioned were strictly complied with; if the attendance of the scholar could be as universal, constant and long contiuned as you have stated; if the teachers were men of those high intellectual and moral qualities, apt to teach and devoted to their work, and favored with that blessing which the word and providence of God teach us always to expect on our honest, earnest, and well-directed efforts in so good a cause; on these conditions and under these circumstances, I do not hesitate to express the opinion that the failures need not be—would not be—*one per cent.*" Miss Catharine A. Beecher, after having been engaged directly and personally as a teacher about fifteen years in Hartford, Connecticut, and Cincinnati, Ohio, with pupils from every State in the Union, after premising that her "chief hope of success would rest on the proper application of those truths and motives which distinguish the teachings of Jesus Christ," says: "I will now suppose that it could be so arranged that in a given place all the children at the age of four years shall be placed six hours a day, for twelve years, under the care of teachers having the same views that I have, and having received that course of training for the office that any State in this Union can secure to the teachers of its children; let it be so arranged that all the children shall remain till sixteen under these teachers, and also that they shall spend their lives in this city, and I have no hesitation in saying I do not believe that one—*no, not a single one*—would fail of proving a prosperous and respectable member of society. Nay, more—I believe every one would, at the close of life, find admission into the world of endless peace and love. I say this solemnly, deliberately, and with the full belief that I am upheld by such imperfect experimental trials as I have made, or seen made by others; but, more than this, that I am sustained by the authority of Heaven, which sets forth this grand palladium of education, 'Train up a child in the way he should go, and when he is old he will not depart from it.'"

What is the legitimate inference from these strong convictions and clear illustrations of the most competent judges and most unexceptionable witnesses, accompanied as they are by the most indubitable and well-attested facts, showing demonstratively the intimate connection which subsists on the one hand between education and virtue, honor and usefulness, and on the other between ignorance and vice, crime, destitution and pauperism?

Is it not clearly and unquestionably shown that the highest and most direct interest of the whole community, and of every individual composing it, demands that the education of its youth should not only be free and universal, but that no pains or expense should be spared to render it thorough and complete—not in intellectual instruction merely—not in the mere communication of knowledge or the advancement of science, however comprehensive or exalted — but, together with this, in that early inclination and that assiduous development, discipline and culture of the heart, the affections, the principles, habits and conduct of life which Christianity inculcates — which a sound and enlightened moral sentiment requires—which reason and philosophy alike dictate—and which every consideration pertaining to the welfare and improvement of society and the advancement of our common humanity imperatively demands.

www.ingramcontent.com/pod-product-compliance
Lightning Source LLC
LaVergne TN
LVHW010249110826
845151LV00004B/1429

* 9 7 8 1 4 2 5 5 2 2 1 6 2 *